First World War
and Army of Occupation
War Diary
France, Belgium and Germany

15 DIVISION
44 Infantry Brigade
Seaforth Highlanders (Ross-shire Buffs, the Duke of Albany's)
8th Battalion
1 October 1916 - 31 December 1916

WO95/1939/4

The Naval & Military Press Ltd
www.nmarchive.com
Published in association with The National Archives

Published by

The Naval & Military Press Ltd

Unit 10 Ridgewood Industrial Park,

Uckfield, East Sussex,

TN22 5QE England

Tel: +44 (0) 1825 749494

www.naval-military-press.com

www.nmarchive.com

This diary has been reprinted in facsimile from the original. Any imperfections are inevitably reproduced and the quality may fall short of modern type and cartographic standards.

© Crown Copyright
Images reproduced by permission of The National Archives, London, England, 2015.

Contents

Document type	Place/Title	Date From	Date To
Heading	War Diary of 8th Service Battalion Seaforth Highlanders. From 1st October 1916 to 31st October 1916 Volume (XVI)		
War Diary	Franvillers	01/10/1916	06/10/1916
War Diary	Becourt Wood	07/10/1916	08/10/1916
War Diary	Martintrench	09/10/1916	10/10/1916
War Diary	Crescent Alley	11/10/1916	12/10/1916
War Diary	26th Avenue	13/10/1916	13/10/1916
War Diary	26th Avenue 1/20000 57 C S.W.	13/10/1916	13/10/1916
War Diary	26th Avenue	14/10/1916	15/10/1916
War Diary	Martinpuich	16/10/1916	16/10/1916
War Diary	Martinpuich 1/2000 57e S.W.	15/10/1916	15/10/1916
War Diary	Bazentine Le Petit	19/10/1916	21/10/1916
War Diary	Martin Trench	22/10/1916	24/10/1916
War Diary	26th Avenue	25/10/1916	26/10/1916
War Diary	Crescent Alley	27/10/1916	28/10/1916
War Diary	Contalmaison	29/10/1916	31/10/1916
Miscellaneous	8th Service Battalion Seaforth Highlanders.	31/10/1916	31/10/1916
Miscellaneous	O.C. All Coys. Appendix I	01/10/1916	01/10/1916
Miscellaneous	O.C. All Coys. Appendix II	02/10/1916	02/10/1916
Miscellaneous	O.C. C		
Operation(al) Order(s)	Operation Order No. 33. by Lieut. Col. G.A. Thomas DSO Commdg 8th Battn Seaforth Highlrs. Appendix III	04/10/1916	04/10/1916
Miscellaneous	O.C. All Coys. Appendix IV	04/10/1916	04/10/1916
Miscellaneous	O.C. All Coys. Appendix V	05/10/1915	05/10/1915
Miscellaneous	A Form. Messages And Signals. App VI		
Operation(al) Order(s)	44th Infantry Brigade Operation Order. No. 2 Appendix VI	04/10/1916	04/10/1916
Map	Appendix VI		
Operation(al) Order(s)	44th Infantry Brigade Operation Order No. 98 Appendix VII	04/10/1916	04/10/1916
Miscellaneous	March Table to accompany 44th Infantry Brigade Operation Order No. 98		
Miscellaneous	All Recipients. of O.O. 33.d/4/X/1916 Appendix VII	05/10/1916	05/10/1916
Operation(al) Order(s)	Operation Order No. 33. by Lieut. Col G.A. Thomson DSO Commdg 8th Battn Seaforth Highlrs.	04/10/1916	04/10/1916
Miscellaneous	44th Brigade B.M. 31. Appendix VIII	05/10/1916	05/10/1916
Miscellaneous	A Form. Messages And Signals.		
Operation(al) Order(s)	44th Infantry Brigade Operation Order No. 99 Appendix X	08/10/1916	08/10/1916
Miscellaneous	Table to accompany 44th Infantry Brigade Operation Order No. 99		
Miscellaneous	44th Brigade B.M. 31. Appendix X	09/10/1916	09/10/1916
Operation(al) Order(s)	44th Infantry Brigade Operation Order No. 100. Appendix XI	10/10/1916	10/10/1916
Miscellaneous	Operation Order No. 34 by Lieut Col G.A. Thomson DSO Commdg 8th Seaforth Highlanders.	10/10/1916	10/10/1916
Miscellaneous	C Form (Original). Messages And Signals. Appendix XIII		

Miscellaneous	C Form (Duplicate). Messages And Signals. Appendix XIII		
Miscellaneous	44th Brigade. B.M. 28. Appendix XIII	11/10/1916	11/10/1916
Miscellaneous	O.C. A Company	11/10/1916	11/10/1916
Miscellaneous	A Form. Messages And Signals.		
Operation(al) Order(s)	44th Infantry Brigade Operation Order No. 101 Appendix XIV	11/10/1916	11/10/1916
Operation(al) Order(s)	Operation Order No. 35. Appendix XVI	12/10/1916	12/10/1916
Operation(al) Order(s)	44th Infantry Brigade Operation Order No. 102. Appendix XV	12/10/1916	12/10/1916
Operation(al) Order(s)	Operation Order by Lieut. Colonel C.H. March DSO. Commanding 7th (Service) Battalions Cameron Highlanders. Appendix XVII	12/10/1916	12/10/1916
Miscellaneous	44th Brigade. B.M. 31. Appendix XVIII	13/10/1916	13/10/1916
Miscellaneous	44th Brigade. R.B. 31 Appendix XIA	14/10/1916	14/10/1916
Miscellaneous	15th Div. 100/11 G.a. Appendix XX	16/10/1916	16/10/1916
Operation(al) Order(s)	44th Infantry Brigade Operation Order No. 104	18/10/1916	18/10/1916
Miscellaneous	Table To Accompany 44th Infantry Brigade Operation Order No. 104 dated 18th October 1916		
Miscellaneous	All Units 44th Inf. Bde. Warning Orders.		
Operation(al) Order(s)	Operation Order No. 36 by Lieut. Col. M.G.S. Thomason DSO Commdg 8th Battn Seaforth Highlanders.	18/10/1916	18/10/1916
Operation(al) Order(s)	44th Infantry Brigade Operation Order No. 105 Appendix XXIII	21/10/1916	21/10/1916
Miscellaneous	44th Brigade B.M. C1. Appendix XXIV	22/10/1916	22/10/1916
Miscellaneous			
Miscellaneous	Work 44th Inf Bde. Appendix XXV	23/10/1916	23/10/1916
Miscellaneous	Operation Order No. 38 Appendix XXVI	24/10/1916	24/10/1916
Operation(al) Order(s)	44th Infantry Brigade Operation Order No. 108. Appendix XXVII	24/10/1916	24/10/1916
Miscellaneous	44th Brigade B.M. 31	24/10/1916	24/10/1916
Miscellaneous			
Miscellaneous	44th Brigade B.M. 28/1	24/10/1916	24/10/1916
Miscellaneous	Liable to Alterations.		
Operation(al) Order(s)	44th Infantry Brigade Operation Order No. 111 Appendix XXX	26/10/1916	26/10/1916
Operation(al) Order(s)	Operation Order No. 39 Lt Col N.A. Thomson DSO. Commdg 8/Seaforth Highrs	26/10/1916	26/10/1916
Miscellaneous	44th Brigade. B.M. 31 Appendix XXXVI	14/04/1917	14/04/1917
Miscellaneous	Appendix XXXIII	26/10/1916	26/10/1916
Operation(al) Order(s)	46th Infantry Brigade Order No. 115 Appendix XXXIV	28/10/1916	28/10/1916
Map	Trench Map		
Miscellaneous			
Heading	War Diary of 8th (Service) Battalion Seaforth Highlanders. from 1st Nov. 1916 to 30th Nov 1916 Volume 7		
War Diary	Contalmaison	01/11/1916	01/11/1916
War Diary	Becaurt	02/11/1916	05/11/1916
War Diary	Bresle	06/11/1916	30/11/1916
Miscellaneous	Appendix I	31/10/1916	31/10/1916
Miscellaneous	46th Infantry Brigade Order No. 119 Appendix II	01/11/1916	01/11/1916
Miscellaneous	March Table. issued with 46th Infantry Brigade Order No. 119 Appendix II		
Miscellaneous			

Miscellaneous	C Form (Duplicate). Messages And Signals. Appendix III		
Miscellaneous			
Miscellaneous	O.C. 8th Seaforth. Working Party. Appendix IV	03/11/1916	03/11/1916
Operation(al) Order(s)	44th Infantry Brigade Operation Order No. 119. Appendix V	04/11/1916	04/11/1916
Miscellaneous	March Table To Accompany 44th Infantry Brigade O.O. No. 119		
Miscellaneous	44th Brigade. B.M. 28. Appendix V	04/11/1916	04/11/1916
Operation(al) Order(s)	Operation Order No. 43. Appendix VI	04/11/1916	04/11/1916
Miscellaneous	8th (S) Battalion Seaforth Highlanders Training Programme for Week Ending November 12th 1916		
Miscellaneous	C Form (Duplicate). Messages And Signals.		
Miscellaneous	8th Battalion Seaforth Highlanders Training Programme Week Ending Nov 18th 1916	11/11/1916	11/11/1916
Miscellaneous	8th Battn Seaforth Highlanders Training Programme Week Ending November 26th 1916		
Miscellaneous	C Form. (Original). Messages And Signals. Appendix XI		
Miscellaneous	C Form. (Original). Messages And Signals. Appendix XII		
Miscellaneous	C Form. (Original). Messages And Signals. Appendix XIII		
Miscellaneous	8th Battalion Seaforth Highlanders. Appendix XIV		
Miscellaneous	Programme 44th "Highland" Brigade Games. to be held on 21st Novbr., 1916 Appendix XV		
Miscellaneous	C Form (Duplicate). Messages And Signals. Appendix XVI		
Miscellaneous	8th Battalion Seaforth Highlanders Training Programme for Week Ending Dec 2nd 1916 Appendix XI	25/11/1916	25/11/1916
Miscellaneous	44th Brigade B.M. 29/6 Appendix XVIII	25/11/1916	25/11/1916
Miscellaneous	8th Battalion Seaforth Highlanders Appendix XIX	16/11/1916	16/11/1916
Miscellaneous	Inspection of 44th Infantry Brigade by G.O.C., 15th Division. Monday 27th Nov. 1916 Appendix XX	26/11/1916	26/11/1916
Miscellaneous	8th Battalions Seaforth Highlanders.	30/11/1916	30/11/1916
Heading	War Diary. 8th (Ser) Battalion Seaforth Highlanders. from 1st Dec 1916 to 31st Dec 1916 Volume 18		
Miscellaneous	Headquarters. 15th Division.	31/12/1916	31/12/1916
War Diary	Bresle	01/12/1916	01/12/1916
War Diary	Albert	02/12/1916	07/12/1916
War Diary	X 2.3 Central	08/12/1916	16/12/1916
War Diary	Shelter Wood	17/12/1916	19/12/1916
War Diary	26th Avenue	20/12/1916	23/12/1916
War Diary	Acid Drop South	24/12/1916	25/12/1916
War Diary	26th Avenue	26/12/1916	27/12/1916
War Diary	Shelter Wood South	28/12/1916	31/12/1916
Miscellaneous	Casualties during the month of December 1916	31/12/1916	31/12/1916
Operation(al) Order(s)	44th Infantry Brigade Operation Order No. 120. Appendix I	02/11/1916	02/11/1916
Miscellaneous	March Table to accompany 44th Infantry Brigade Operation Order No. 120 dated 28.11.16		
Operation(al) Order(s)	Operation Order No. 44 by Lieut. Col N.A. Thomson D.S.O. Commdg 8th (S) Battahaz Seaforth Highlanders. Appendix II	30/11/1916	30/11/1916
Miscellaneous	Headquarters, 8th Seaforth Hrs. Appendix III	30/11/1916	30/11/1916
Miscellaneous	O.C. All Coys. Quartermaster Appendix IV	01/12/1916	01/12/1916

Miscellaneous	44th Brigade B.M. 31/16 Appendix V	01/12/1916	01/12/1916
Miscellaneous	O.C. All Coys. Signalling Officer. Appendix VI	01/12/1916	01/12/1916
Miscellaneous	O.C. All Coys. Appendix VII	01/12/1916	01/12/1916
Miscellaneous	8th Seaforth Highlanders Training Programme Week Ending Dec 9th 1916 Appendix VIII		
Miscellaneous	O.C. All Coys. Appendix IX	02/12/1916	02/12/1916
Miscellaneous	Appendix X O.C. All Coys. Appendix X	03/12/1916	03/12/1916
Miscellaneous	O.C. All Coys. Appendix XI		
Miscellaneous	15th Division. No. 108/G.a. Appendix XI	03/12/1916	03/12/1916
Miscellaneous	O.C. All Coys. Appendix XII	04/12/1916	04/12/1916
Miscellaneous	44th Brigade. Appendix XI.	04/12/1916	04/12/1916
Miscellaneous	All Battns. 44th I.B. Appendix XIV	03/12/1916	03/12/1916
Miscellaneous	O.C. All Coy's Appendix XV	05/12/1916	05/12/1916
Operation(al) Order(s)	44th Infantry Brigade Operation Order No. 121 Appendix XVI	05/12/1916	05/12/1916
Miscellaneous	Relief Table to accompany 44th Infantry Brigade Operation Order No. 121 d/5.12.16		
Miscellaneous	Addendum No. 1 to 44th Inf. Bde. Operation Order No. 121 dated 5th December 1916 Appendix XVI	06/12/1916	06/12/1916
Miscellaneous	44th Brigade. S.C. 17/106 App XVI	06/12/1916	06/12/1916
Operation(al) Order(s)	Operation Order No. 45. by Lieut. Col. N.A. Thomson D.S.O. Commdg 8th Seaforth Highlrs Appendix XVII	06/12/1916	06/12/1916
Miscellaneous	Appendix XVIII	07/11/1916	07/11/1916
Miscellaneous	15th Division No. 107/G.a. Appendix XVIII	07/12/1916	07/12/1916
Miscellaneous	44th Brigade. B.M. 33. Appendix XIX	06/12/1916	06/12/1916
Miscellaneous	44th Brigade. B.M. 33 Appendix XIX	07/12/1916	07/12/1916
Operation(al) Order(s)	44th Infantry Brigade Operation Order No. 122. Appendix XX	14/12/1916	14/12/1916
Miscellaneous	March Table of reliefs on 16th December 1916 issued with 44th Infantry Brigade Operation Order No. 122 dated 14th December 1916		
Miscellaneous	Addendum No. 1 to 44th Infantry Brigade Operation Order No. 122. List of working parties to be found by 44th Infantry Brigade when in the Line.		
Miscellaneous	C Form (Original). Messages And Signals.		
Operation(al) Order(s)	Operation Order No. 46 by Lieut. Col. N.H. Thomson D.S.O. Commdg 8th Battn. Seaforth Highlanders. Appendix XXI	15/12/1916	15/12/1916
Miscellaneous	44th Brigade. S.C. 11/46. Appendix XXII	15/12/1916	15/12/1916
Miscellaneous	Working Carrying Party. Appendix XXIII	16/12/1916	16/12/1916
Operation(al) Order(s)	44th Infantry Brigade Operation Order No. 123. Appendix XXIV	18/12/1916	18/12/1916
Miscellaneous	Table to Accompany 44th Infantry Brigade Operation Order No. 123 d/18-12-16		
Operation(al) Order(s)	Operation Order No. 47. by Lieut. Col. N.A. Thomson, D.S.O., Commdg 8th Bn. Seaforth Highlanders. Appendix XXV		
Operation(al) Order(s)	Operation Order No. 2. Appendix XXVI	18/12/1916	18/12/1916
Miscellaneous	44th Brigade B.M. 269/1		
Operation(al) Order(s)	44th Infantry Brigade Operation Order No. 124. Appendix XXVIII	21/12/1916	21/12/1916
Operation(al) Order(s)	Operation Order No. 48 Appendix XXIX	21/12/1916	21/12/1916
Miscellaneous	A Form. Messages And Signals. Appendix XX		
Miscellaneous	A Form. Messages And Signals.		
Operation(al) Order(s)	Operation Order No. 49. by Lieut Com N.A. Thomson D.S.O. Commdg 8th Seaforth	22/12/1916	22/12/1916

Operation(al) Order(s)	44th Infantry Brigade Operation Order No. 125. Appendix XXXII	22/12/1916	22/12/1916
Operation(al) Order(s)	Operation Order No. 50 Appendix XXXIII	23/12/1916	23/12/1916
Operation(al) Order(s)	44th Infantry Brigade Operation Order No. 126 Appendix XXXIV	21/12/1916	21/12/1916
Operation(al) Order(s)	Operation Order No. 51 Appendix XXXV		
Operation(al) Order(s)	7th (S) Battalion Cameron High Operation Orders No. 7 Appendix 36	25/12/1916	25/12/1916
Operation(al) Order(s)	Operation Order No. 52 by Major U.P. Swinburne Commdg 8th Seaforth Hrs Appendix XXXVI	26/12/1916	26/12/1916
Operation(al) Order(s)	44th Infantry Brigade Operation Order No. 127 Appendix XXXVII	26/12/1916	26/12/1916
Miscellaneous	Relief Table to accompany 44th Infantry Brigade operation Order No. 127		
Operation(al) Order(s)	44th Infantry Brigade Operation Order No. 128. Appendix XL	30/12/1916	30/12/1916
Miscellaneous	Table to accompany 44th Infantry Brigade Operation Order No. 128 d/30-12-16		
Operation(al) Order(s)	Operation Order No. 54 by Major U.P. Swinburne Commdg 8th Seaforth Highlanders Appendix	30/12/1916	30/12/1916

CONFIDENTIAL

WAR DIARY
of
8th Service Battalion Seaforth Highlanders.

From- 1st October, 1916. to- 31st October, 1916.

VOLUME
(XVI)

In the Field.
31-10-1916.

Jen Thomson
......................Lt Colonel.
Comdg; 8th. Service Battalion Seaforth Highlanders.

Army Form C. 2118.

WAR DIARY
or
INTELLIGENCE SUMMARY.
(Erase heading not required.)

Instructions regarding War Diaries and Intelligence Summaries are contained in F. S. Regs., Part II. and the Staff Manual respectively. Title pages will be prepared in manuscript.

Place	Date	Hour	Summary of Events and Information	Remarks and references to Appendices
FRANVILLERS	1/10/16		Church Parades were held in the forenoon	
FRANVILLERS	2/10/16		Training carried out as per attached programme	Appendix I
FRANVILLERS	3/10/16		The Battalion Route marched as per attached order. Route BONNAY, HEILLY, FRANVILLERS. Major Gillatt joined the Battalion as 2nd in command. attached from 13 Bn. The Royal Scots	Appendix II
FRANVILLERS	4/10/16		Battalion ordered to move to BECOURT WOOD as per attached order. This order was subsequently cancelled	Appendix III
FRANVILLERS	5/10/16		In the forenoon Conferences were at the disposal of Coy. commanders for kit inspections etc. The Battalion paraded at 1.40 p.m. under the Commanding Officer for the rehearsal of an attack under Brigade arrangements	Appendix IV Appendix V Appendix VI

WAR DIARY
or
INTELLIGENCE SUMMARY.
(Erase heading not required.)

Army Form C. 2118.

Place	Date	Hour	Summary of Events and Information	Remarks and references to Appendices
RANVILLERS	6/10/16		The Battalion moved to BECOURT WOOD in accordance with Bgde operation order no 98 originally issued for execution on 4th inst. Working party of 300 O.R. ordered for work on roads near CONTALMAISON. This order was subsequently cancelled. JJB	appendix VII appendix VIII
BECOURT WOOD	7/10/16		Battalion H.Q.As remained in BECOURT WOOD. "A" & "B" Coys lent to the 69th Brigade and "C" & "D" Coys to the 68th Brigade for carrying purposes only in the vicinity of MARTINPUICH. Casualties Wounded 5 O.R. Missing 1 O.R. JJB	

Army, Form C. 2118.

WAR DIARY
or
INTELLIGENCE SUMMARY.
(Erase heading not required.)

Instructions regarding War Diaries and Intelligence Summaries are contained in F.S. Regs., Part II. and the Staff Manual respectively. Title pages will be prepared in manuscript.

Place	Date	Hour	Summary of Events and Information	Remarks and references to Appendices
BECOURT WOOD	8/10/16		Battalion moved up to relieve 10th Bn. Northumberland Fusiliers. The Coys being closely followed on carrying fatigue were not brought back to BECOURT. "B" Coy & three platoons of "A" Coy moved into MARTIN TRENCH. "C" & "D" Coys and one platoon of "A" Coy moved into Stafford TRENCH. Battalion H.Qrs in MARTIN TRENCH at junction of CRESCENT ALLEY at M32 d.4.6. Brigade O.O. no 99. Permanent carrying party of 25 O.R. to work under 73rd Field Coy R.E. Casualties wounded 4 O.R. Missing 2 O.R. EYB	Appendix IV Appendix X
MARTIN TRENCH	9/10/16		Battalion remained in the same position. Working party of 52. EYB	
MARTIN TRENCH	10/10/16		Battalion again in the same positions. Working party of 10 for revetting purposes reported at Brigade H.Qrs. In accordance with operation orders the Battalion proceeded to take over from the 7th Bn. Cameron Highlanders in support. "A" & "C" Coys in PRUE TRENCH "B" Coy in CRESCENT ALLEY & "D" Coy in O.G.I. Brigade D.D. no 100 Batn " " 34	Appendix XI Appendix XII

Army Form C. 2118.

WAR DIARY
or
INTELLIGENCE SUMMARY.
(Erase heading not required.)

Instructions regarding War Diaries and Intelligence Summaries are contained in F. S. Regs., Part II. and the Staff Manual respectively. Title pages will be prepared in manuscript.

Place	Date	Hour	Summary of Events and Information	Remarks and references to Appendices
MARTIN TRENCH	10/10/16 (cont)	11.30 AM	Btn. Hqrs. removed to CRESCENT ALLEY at M.27.b.9.2.	Appendix
CRESCENT ALLEY	11/10/16	4.30 AM	Relief reported complete. During the day work & parties under Btn arrangements. Casualties killed 1 O.R. wounded 3 O.R.	Appendix
CRESCENT ALLEY	12/10/16	7 AM 6.05 P.M.	Bombardment of enemy positions and trenches. In connection with an attack by the 9th Divn. before zero.	Appendix XIII Appendix XIV Appendix XV
		12 MN.	The Btn. relieved the 7th Btn. Cameron Hldrs. in the front line trenches of L.E. SARS. A Coy in left firing line. D Coy in right firing line. "C" Coy in sunken road & TANGLE TRENCHES. A Coy in O.G.2. Btn. HQrs. removed to 26th AVENUE about M.22.a.2.0. Casualties killed 1 O.R. wounded 4 O.R.	Appendix XVI & XVII
26th AVENUE	13/10/16	2.35 AM	Relief of 7th Camerons reported complete	
		3.15 AM	Barrage received from the Divn. on our right about the South of [illegible]/head	

WAR DIARY or INTELLIGENCE SUMMARY

Army Form C. 2118.

Place	Date	Hour	Summary of Events and Information	Remarks and references to Appendices
R.L. AVENUE 57ᵈ S.W.	13-10-16 (cont.)	3.15pm	had established a post about M.16.d.6.43 and asking us to get in touch with them and to link up with strong points to their position. 2nd Lt Sherwood sent with instructions to O.C. "D" Coy. to act in accordance with this request to establish one or more strong points according to circumstances on a line running approximately through M.16.d.2.7	Appendix XVIII
		7.30pm	O.C. "D" Coy reported that he had been unable to get in touch with the South Africans on our right and it subsequently transpired that the enemy was in possession of the strong point at M.16.d.6.4½	
		2.30pm	Received instructions to have a communication trench tapied out through the orchard to front line trench & running approximately M.16.c.1½.3.½ M.16.c.3.8. M.16.a.5.3. to M.16.a central a distance of about 600 yds in all. A working party of 300 of the 9th Gordons to be supplied; he report at Btn H.Qrs at 7.30 P.M. Only ½ or ¼ a working party reported & work was interrupted by shelling. 90 yds of trench were dug and cleared and 250 yds of the new trench dug to an average depth of 4 ft 6 in. Three parties of the 179th the Saxon Regiment came over and surrendered	

Army Form C. 2118.

WAR DIARY
or
INTELLIGENCE SUMMARY.
(Erase heading not required.)

Place	Date	Hour	Summary of Events and Information	Remarks and references to Appendices
6th AVENUE 20.000 57°S.W.	13.10.16 (cont)		Thereabouts to 2nd Lt. Wilson of "B" Coy. "B" & "D" Coy. got in touch with each other about M.16.b.3.4. & dug themselves in to the Bapaume Road at this point. Casualties Officers wounded 2 — 2nd Lt Potter W.H. & 2nd Lt McAskie A. O.R. killed 2. Wounded 19. YAS	
6th AVENUE	14.10.16		Battalion endeavored to hold the front line. Communication trench through the orchard carried forward to the edge of the orchard a further distance of 250 yds. work again done by the 9th Inniskillings but trench taped out by our "B" Coy officers. "B" Coy supplied a party of 20 men for the purpose of tunnelling road at 16.b.2.25. Work in charge of R.E. Instructions re consolidation of line received. YAS Casualties Killed 4 O.R. Wounded 31 O.R.	Appendix XIX Appendix XX
6th AVENUE	15.10.16		Battalion was relieved in the front trenches by the 10th Bn Cameronians in accordance with operation orders No.103 MARTINPUICH	
		10.15 P.M.	Battalion H.Qrs moved to Quadrangle at a point M.33.a.1.9. "A" Coy in TYNE dugouts /gmgh	

T2134. Wt. W708—776. 500000. 4/16. Sir J. C. & S.

Army Form C. 2118.

WAR DIARY
or
INTELLIGENCE SUMMARY.
(Erase heading not required.)

Instructions regarding War Diaries and Intelligence Summaries are contained in F.S. Regs., Part II. and the Staff Manual respectively. Title pages will be prepared in manuscript.

Place	Date	Hour	Summary of Events and Information	Remarks and references to Appendices
26th AVENUE (cont-)	15/10/16	10.15 P.M	Trenches "B & D" in STARFISH and "C" in PRUE TRENCH. Casualties killed 5 O.R. Wounded 10 O.R. 44A	
MARTINPUICH	16/10/16		Battalion remained in the same position. 44A	
MARTINPUICH	17/10/16	1.30 A.M	Four new officers joined from the reinforcement Camp - 2nd Lt. Rutherford J.A. 2nd Lt. Lothian D.E. 2nd Lt. McLeod D.f. 2nd Lt. McLeod A. Battalion remained in the same position. Casualties wounded 1 O.R. 44A	

T2134. Wt. W708—776. 500000. 4/15. Sir J. C. & S.

Army Form C. 2118.

WAR DIARY
or
INTELLIGENCE SUMMARY.
(Erase heading not required.)

Instructions regarding War Diaries and Intelligence Summaries are contained in F.S. Regs., Part II. and the Staff Manual respectively. Title pages will be prepared in manuscript.

Place	Date	Hour	Summary of Events and Information	Remarks and references to Appendices
MARTINPUICH 2000 sq. 57e S.W.	16/10/16		Battalion had use of Divisional Baths at BECOURT in accordance with O.O. no 104. The Battalion moved to trenches vacated by the	Appendix XXI & XXII
		7.15 p.m	8/10th Gordons in the vicinity of BAZENTINE LE PETIT. Battalion HQrs moved to a point about S.9.a.8.3. "A" + "C" Coys in SWANSEA trench "B" in O.G. I + "D" in COURLAY trench.	44B
BAZENTINE LE PETIT	19/10/16		Battalion remained in position. Working parties ordered were subsequently cancelled on account of the weather.	44B
BAZENTINE LE PETIT	20/10/16		Battalion remained in position. Casualties. Wounded 1 O.R.	44B

T2134. Wt. W708—776. 500000. 4/15. Sir J. C. & S.

WAR DIARY
or
INTELLIGENCE SUMMARY.
(Erase heading not required.)

Army Form C. 2118.

Place	Date	Hour	Summary of Events and Information	Remarks and references to Appendices
BAZENTINE LE PETIT	21/10/16		In accordance with Brigade O.O. no 105 the Bn. relieved the 7th Dr. Cameron Highlanders in 2nd Support in PRUE, MARTIN & STARFISH TRENCHES, Bn HQrs. at junction of MARTIN TRENCH with CRESCENT ALLEY JYB	Appendix XXIII
MARTIN TRENCH	22/10/16		In accordance with 44th Bgde B.M. 31 a working party of 4 officers & 200 men covered work at 7 P.M. on digging & improving jumping off trenches as detailed in the order JYB	Appendix XXIV
MARTIN TRENCH	23/10/16		In accordance with Bgde. instructions a working party of 4 officers & 200 men covered work at midnight on digging and improving trenches as detailed in order Casualties Wounded 1 O.R. JYB	Appendix XXV

Army Form C. 2118.

WAR DIARY
or
INTELLIGENCE SUMMARY.
(Erase heading not required.)

Place	Date	Hour	Summary of Events and Information	Remarks and references to Appendices
MARTIN TRENCH	24/10/16		Battalion relieved the 9th Bn. Black Watch in the front system. "A" Coy. in left firing line, "C" Coy. on right firing line, "D" Coy. in support in the CUTTING and "B" Coy. in reserve in O.G.1. Working party supplied in accordance with 44 A.gl BM 31	Appendix XXVI Appendix XXVII Appendix XXVIII
		6:30 p.m.	Btn. H.Qrs. moved to 26th AVENUE 44B	
26th AVENUE	25/10/16		Battalion remained in front system	Appendix XXIX Appendix XXX XXXVI 2nd
			Casualties killed 1 O.R. Wounded 3 O.R. Missing 4 O.R. 34B	
26th AVENUE	26/10/16		Battalion relieved in the front system by the 12th Btn. H.L.I. "A" & "C" Coys. moved to CRESCENT ALLEY and "D" to O.G.1 "B" Coy. to PRUE TRENCH. Working party of 2 officers + 100 men supplied to dig jumping off trench M16 b 0 ½ c to M16 b 5.5.	Appendix XXX + XXXI Appendix XXXII + XXXIII
			Casualties wounded 2 O.R. 44B	

Army Form C. 2118.

WAR DIARY
or
INTELLIGENCE SUMMARY.
(Erase heading not required.)

Instructions regarding War Diaries and Intelligence Summaries are contained in F. S. Regs., Part II. and the Staff Manual respectively. Title pages will be prepared in manuscript.

Place	Date	Hour	Summary of Events and Information	Remarks and references to Appendices
CRESCENT ALLEY	27/10/16		Battalion remained in position. GYB	
CRESCENT ALLEY	28/10/16		Battalion remained in position till this afternoon when in accordance with Bgde OO no 115 they proceeded to take over from the 15th Scottish Rifles in CONTALMAISON. On completion of relief the Bn. came under command of the 46th Inf. Bgde. GYB	appendix XXXIV
CONTALMAISON	29/10/16		Battalion remained in CONTALMAISON. GYB	
CONTALMAISON	30/10/16		Battalion remained in CONTALMAISON. GYB	

T2134. Wt. W708—776. 500000. 4/15. Sir J. C. & S.

Army Form C. 2118.

WAR DIARY
or
INTELLIGENCE SUMMARY.
(Erase heading not required.)

Instructions regarding War Diaries and Intelligence Summaries are contained in F. S. Regs., Part II. and the Staff Manual respectively. Title pages will be prepared in manuscript.

Place	Date	Hour	Summary of Events and Information	Remarks and references to Appendices
CONTALMAISON	3/10/16		Battalion remained in CONTALMAISON. 44A	

8th Service Battalion Seaforth Highlanders.

CASUALTIES DURING THE MONTH OF OCTOBER, 1916.

OFFICERS.

2/Lieut. W.M. POTTER.   Wounded in Action, 13/10/1916.
2/Lieut. A. McADIE.   Wounded in Action, 13/10/1916.

OTHER RANKS.

KILLED.

11th October	Total=	1.
13th October	"	2.
14th October	"	4.
15th October	"	5.
12th October	"	1.
25th October	"	1.
	Total=	14

OTHER RANKS

WOUNDED.

7th October	Total=	5.
8th October	"	4.
11th October	"	3.
12th October	"	4.
13th October	"	19.
14th October	"	31.
15th October	"	10.
17th October	"	1.
20th October	"	1.
23rd October	"	1.
25th October	"	3.
26th October	"	2.
	Total	84.

OTHER RANKS.

MISSING.

7th October	Total=	1.
8th October	"	2.
25th October	"	1
	Total=	4

GRAND TOTAL.		Officers.	Other Ranks.
	Killed.	Nil.	14.
	Wounded.	2.	84.
	Missing.	Nil.	4

In the Field.
31-10-1916.

_____ Captain.
Adjutant, 8th Bn. Seaforth Highlanders.

D.595/9.

O.C.All Coys.
Lewis Gun Officer.
Pioneer Officer.
44th I.Bde(for information)

Appendix I

1. Training to-morrow will be as follows:-

   (a) <u>From 7.A.M.to 7-45.A.M.</u> Early Morning Parade under Company arrangements.
   All N.C.C's except Company Sergeant-Majors & Company Quartermaster Sergeants will parade outside Bn.Hd.Qrs at 6-50.A.M.under the Regimental Sergeant-Major.
   <u>DRESS.</u>-Rifles,Belts & Sidearms.

   (b) <u>From 9-15.A.M.to 1.P.M.</u> Company Training including Company Drill,Extended Order Drill,Bayonet Fighting & Practice of throwing dummy Grenades.

2. 1.Subaltern1.N.C.O & 19 men per Company will parade outside Bn.Hd Qrs at 8-45.A.M.under 2/Lieut.J.H.Ross.
These parties will each dig a Strong Point of the standard type-2/Lieut J.H.Ross will arrange for necessary material to be drawn from 44th Infantry Brigade Hd Qrsm
4 Instructors from the 73rd Field Coy,R.E.will assist in this work. Tools will be drawn from the Quartermaster Stores.

3. Scouts will train to-morrow under 2/Lieut.D.E.F.C.Hervey.

4. All Lewis Gun Detachments will train under the Lewis Gun Officers.

5. The Lewis Gun Officer will arrange for 2/Lieut Hervey to have the use of one Barr & Stroud Range Finder and for "A" Company to have the use of the other.
"C"Company will have the use of the German Machine Gun.
immediately
6. Training will be in the Fields N & N.W.of FRANVILLERS.

In the Field.
1-10-1916.

George W. Duncan.
..........................Captain.
Adjutant,8th Bn.Seaforth Highlanders.

Appendix II

D 596.

O.C. All Coys.
Lewis Gun Officer.
Pioneer Officer.
44th Infantry Brigade (for information)
----

1. Training to-morrow will be as follows:-

    The Battalion will parade at &Q 9-30.A.M. for Route-Marching under the Commanding Officer.

    Starting Point:- Ref Map 1/40,000 Sheet 63D.
    Forked roads C.29.b.4.0. facing South.
    Platoons will move off at 100 yards interval.

    Route:- Road through C.29.d,I.5.11 & 17 to BONNAY thence to I.24.c.0.3 & thence to HEILLY via J.13.b.e.0.7. Thence to cross roads D.26 central to D.13. c.7.0.& D.13.d.5.5 to FRANVILLERS.

    Order of March:- "C" "D" "A" "B".

    Dress:- Fighting Order, less Packs, Steel Helmets & Khaki Aprons.

2. O.C. "C" Company will detail 1 Subaltern to march with Signallers to guide the Battalion.

3. 1st Line of Transport will not accompany the Battalion on the march.

4. Attendance as for parade as for the 27th ulto.

In the Field.   ....Blackwood....2/Lieut.
2/10/1916.   8th Bn. Seaforth Highlanders.

occ

SECRET

Appendix III
Copy No 11

Operation Order No 33.
by
Lieut. Col. J. A. Thomson DSO
Commdg: 8th Battn Seaforth Highlrs.

4 October 1916.

Reference Map. AMIENS SHEET 1/100,000

1. The Battalion will march to BECOURT today 4th October as follows:-
   STARTING POINT:- Forked Roads 50 yds west of Battn Headquarters.
   TIME:- 1-50 p.m.
   ORDER OF MARCH:- "D", "A", "B", "C" Coys, Headqrs, Lewis Gun Detatchment.
   ROUTE:- AMIENS - ALBERT - BECOURT road.

2. 100 yards interval will be maintained between Platoons and equivalent units.

3. Normal halts at 10 minutes to every hour will be observed.
   Brigade time will be notified between 10 & 11 a.m this morning.

4. 1st Line Transport will march in rear of Battalion.

5. Advanced parties of 1 N.C.O. per Coy & 1 for Headqrs on bicycles will parade at Battn Hqrs at 10.a.m. and proceed to BECOURT CHATEAU where they will meet 2/Lieut J.H. Ross at 1-0 p.m.

6. All blankets and surplus Kits will be taken to Brigade Store at No 154 HIGH STREET by 11-0.a.m.
   Officers Kits going with the Battn will be taken to ~~Brigade~~ Quartermasters' Stores by 1-0.p.m.
   Mess boxes will be collected at 1-30 p.m.

George W. Duncan
Captain
Adjutant: 8th Battn Seaforth Highlanders

Copy No 1 -- O.C. "A" Coy
       2 -- O.C. "B" Coy
       3 -- O.C. "C" Coy
       4 -- O.C. "D" Coy
       5 -- Lewis Gun Officer.
       6 -- Transport Officer.
       7 -- Quartermaster.
       8 -- 2nd in Command.
       9 -- War Diary (Duplicate)
      10 -- File.
      11 -- ~~Duplicate~~ War Diary.

D.597/1.

Appendix IV

O.C. All Coys.
Lewis Gun Officer.
Pioneer Officer
Quartermaster.
44th Inf. Bde - for information.
----

1. Companies will be at the disposal of Company Commanders during to-morrow morning.
   The opportunity should be taken of holding Kit Inspections & completing deficiencies that may be necessary.

2. The Battalion will parade at 1-30.P.M. to-morrow under the Commanding Officer. Further orders as to this parades will be issued later.

In the Field.
4/X/1916.

............................Captain.
Adjutant, 8th Bn. Seaforth Highrs.

Appendix V

O.C. All Coys.
Lewis Gun Officer.
PIONEER Officer.
----

1. The Battalion will parade at 1-40.P.M.to-day in the field at pt C 29.a.9½.8.

2. Markers will report to the Battalion Sergeant-Major at 1-15.P.M. at Bn. Hd Qrs.

3. DRESS:- Fighting Order. Khaki Aprons and Shrapnel Helmets will be worn.
No Bombs and ~~extra~~ Sandbags and no extra ammunition will be carried.
Tools will be issued to Coys this morning.

4. Coys will march to the parade ground independently.

5/X/1916.

............, Captain.
Adjutant. 8th Bn. Seaforth Highlanders.

Attach app VI

"A" Form.
MESSAGES AND SIGNALS.

Army Form C.2121 (in pads of 100).

Prefix ...... Code ...... m.	Words	Charge	This message is on a/c of:	Recd. at ...... m.
Office of Origin and Service Instructions.	Sent At ...... m. To By		...... Service ...... (Signature of "Franking Officer.")	Date From 5.X.16 By

TO: All Units 44th I.B. ~~15th Div.~~

Sender's Number.	Day of Month.	In reply to Number.		
BM 334	5			A A A

Ref 44th Bde O.O. dated 4-10-16 (Scheme) AAA Zero will be at 2-15 PM AAA Addressed all concerned

From 44th I.B.
Place
Time 8-30 am

appendix VI

44th Infantry Brigade Operation Order.   Copy No. 2

4-10-16.

Reference 62D.1/40,000. and
Sketch Map attached.

1. III Corps will continue the attack to-morrow, 5th October, with 47th Division on Right and 15th Division on Left.

   XV Corps will co-operate on right, Canadians on Left.

   15th Division holds the line from C.30.a.2.0. to C.17.d.6.1. 44th Infantry Brigade on the right, 45th Infantry Brigade on the left.

2. 44th Infantry Brigade will capture the German defences – including the village of WARLENCOURT and Fme. ST. LAURENT – and will dig in on the line of the 3rd objective.

   The first objective is German trench line from D.19.c.10.5. to C.24.b.4.3½.

   The second objective – a line drawn through D.19.b.5.3½. to D.19.a.0.10.

   Third objective from D.13.d.8.9½. to 13.a.9½.6.

   Brigade boundaries are shown on attached sketch.

3. 8/10th Gordon Hrs. on the right, and 9th Black Watch on left will deliver the assault.

   7th Cameron Hrs. will be in Brigade Support,
   8th Seaforth Hrs. in Brigade Reserve.

4. Units will be in positions of assembly by 2 P.M. A.M.
   8/10th Gordon Hrs. (now in the line) will close to their right to make room for 9th Black Watch. The two leading companies of each of these battalions will be in the front trench, the third companies in the second trench, and the fourth companies in Battalion reserve.

   7th Cameron Hrs. will be just to the E. of the FRANVILLERS – HEILLY Road north of the main AMIENS – ALBERT Road.

   8th Seaforth Hrs. will be near the FRANVILLERS – BAIZIEUX Road between points C.29.a.9½.8. and 23.c.9½.1.

5. One Stokes Gun with 50 rounds of ammunition will be attached to each of the three leading battalions and be under the orders of the Battalion Commanders.

   2 Vickers Guns will be attached to each battalion and will be under the orders of the Battalion Commanders.

   4 Vickers Guns will be disposed so as to bring indirect fire to bear on roads and lines of advance in rear of Fme. ST. LAURENT.

   4 Vickers Guns will be with the Brigade Reserve at FRANVILLERS.

(2.)

6. The advance will be covered by a creeping barrage which will commence at Zero 150 yards in front of our front line and will advance at the rate of 100 yards a minute.

   A halt of 20 minutes will be made after the capture of the first objective, 30 minutes after the capture of the second objective, and a barrage will be maintained at 100 yards beyond the 3rd objective until ordered to cease.

7. Each battalion will trace out and dig four strong points. 8/10th Gordons and 9th Black Watch on line of 3rd objective, 7th Cameron Hrs. N., N.E., E. & S. of "WARLENCOURT".
   8th Seaforth Hrs. on line of 1st objective.

8. White flags denote a trench line.

   Red flags a strong point.

   Khaki screens machine guns in action. The latter must be knocked out by Stokes before they can be considered as captured.

9. Brigade Signal Officer will establish a visual station in G.29.b. Battalions will maintain communication with this station.

10. Brigade Headquarters will be at FRANVILLERS where all reports will be sent.

                                        Captain,
                                        Brigade Major,
                                        44th Infantry Brigade.
4-10-16.

   Copies to :-
      No. 1. 9th Black Watch.
          2. 8th Seaforths.
          3. 8/10th Gordons.
          4. 7th Camerons.
          5. 44 M.G.Coy.
          6. 44 T.M.Battery.
          7. 15th Div.
          8. 44th Bde.Signals.
          9. War Diary.
         10. File.
         11. Right Bde.) Not issued.
         12. Left.Bde.)

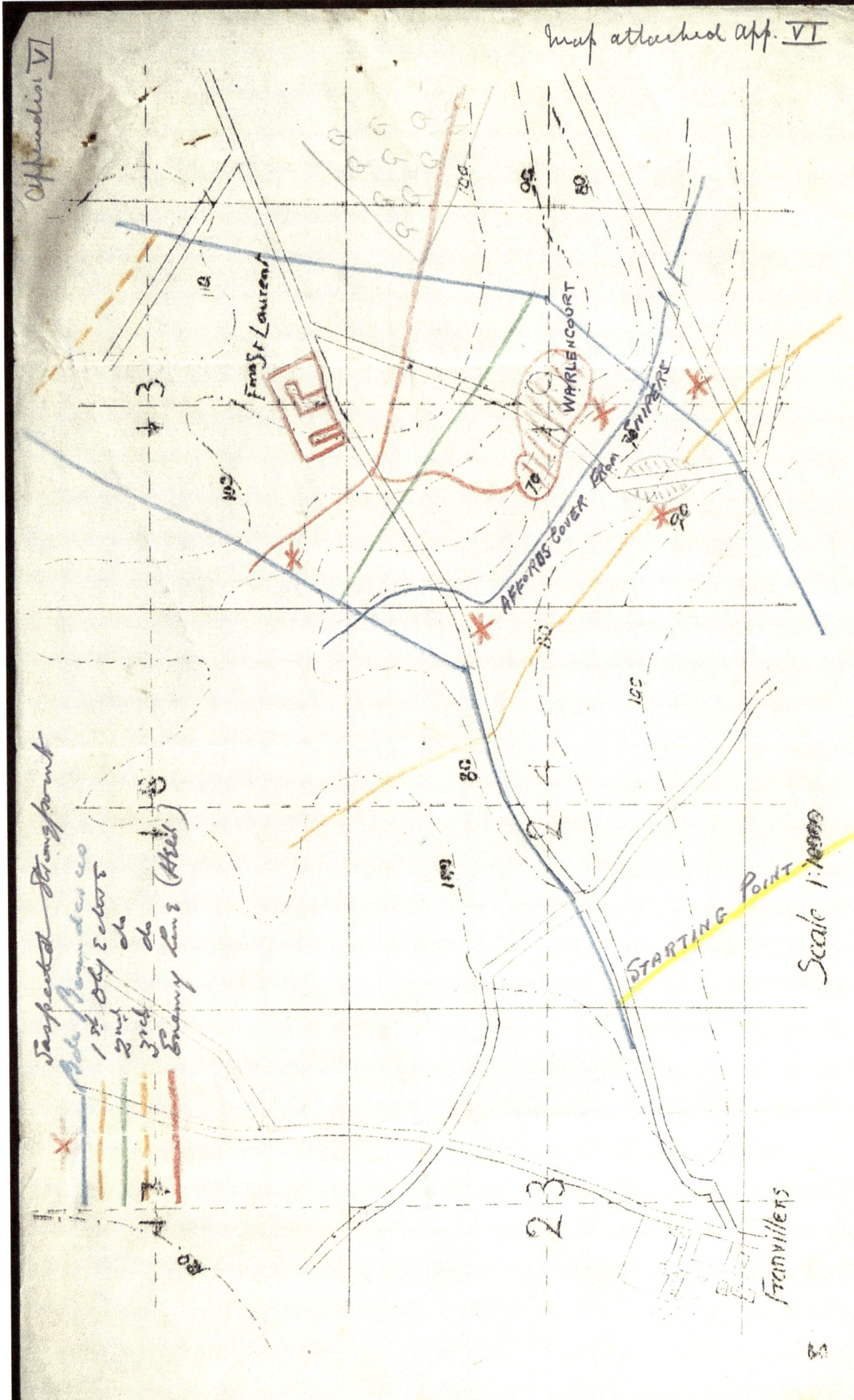

Appendix VII

S E C R E T. Copy No. 2

44th Infantry Brigade Operation Order No.98.

4-10-16.

Reference Map.
AMIENS SHEET 1/100,000.
ALBERT Combined Sheet 1/40,000.

1. The 44th Infantry Brigade will march to-day, 4th October, to BECOURT (distance about 9½ miles) in accordance with the attached March Table.

2. Brigade time will be notified to units between 10 and 11 A.M. October 4th.

3. Transport will march in rear of units.

4. 200 yards distance will be maintained between battalions and 100 yards between platoons and equivalent units.

5. Normal halts will be observed.

6. Advance parties (5 per battalion and 1 per M.G.Coy. and T.M.Battery) on bicycles will meet Staff Captain and their billeting officers at BECOURT CHATEAU at 1 P.M.

7. Working parties at VIVIER SIDING and ST.GRATIEN will remain pending further orders.

8. Reports to the head of the column.
Brigade Headquarters open on arrival at BECOURT.

Kenneth Barge.

Captain,
Brigade Major,
44th Infantry Brigade.

Issued through
Signals.
8-0 A.M.

Copies to :-
1. 9th Black Watch.
2. 8th Seaforth Hrs.
3. 8/10th Gordon Hrs.
4. 7th Cameron Hrs.
5. 44 M.G.Coy.
6. 44 T.M.Battery.
7. H.Q.15th Div.
8.   Inf.Bde.
9. 73rd Fld.Coy.R.E.
10. Town Major, FRANVILLERS.
11. Town Major BECOURT.
12. 47th Fld.Amb.
13. Bde.Transport Offcr.
14. "   Supply Offcr.
15. "   Signal Offcr.
16. No.2 Coy.Train.
17. Staff Captain.
18. War Diary.
19. File

March Table to accompany 44th Infantry Brigade Operation Order No.98.

Units in order of march.	Starting Point. Place.	Time.	Route.	Destination.
1 platoon, 9th Black Watch.	Cross Roads ALBERT - AMIENS, and HEILLY - FRANVILLERS.	P.M. 1-0	AMIENS - ALBERT and BECOURT Road.	BECOURT.
44th I.B.H.Qrs. & Signal Secn:		1-1		
9th Black Watch. (less 1 platoon).		1-4		
44 M.G.Coy.		1-29		
8/10th Gordon Hrs.		1-35		
8th Seaforth Hrs.		2-0		
7th Cameron Hrs.		2-25		
44 T.M.Battery.		2-40		

Appendix VII

SECRET.

D.618.

All Recipients. of O.O.35.d/4/X/1916.

Reference Operation Order No.33.dated 4th October, 1916, the order will hold good for to-morrow 6th October, 1916, with the following exceptions:-

(1) Order of March.—"D" "C" Headquarters, Lewis Guns Coy. Detachments.

(2) Advanced parties of 1.N.C.O per Coy & 1 for Hdqrs will proceed with "A" & "B" Coy's by Bus leaving Brigade Headquarters at 6-30.A.M. and await at BECOURT Chateau until the billeting officer arrives.

George W. Duncan
..................Captain.
Adjutant.6th Bn.Seaforth Highlanders.

In the Field.
5/X/1916.

SECRET

Appendix VII

Operation Order No 33.
by
Lieut. Col. N. A. Thomson DSO
Commdg: 8th Battn Seaforth Highlrs.

Copy No 9

4 October 1916.

Reference Map. AMIENS SHEET 1/100,000

1. The Battalion will march to BECOURT today 4th October as follows:-
   STARTING POINT:- Forked Roads 50 yds west of Battn Headquarters.
   TIME :- 1-50 p.m.
   ORDER of MARCH :- "D", "A", "B", "C" Coys, Headqrs Lewis Gun Detatchment.
   ROUTE :- AMIENS – ALBERT – BECOURT road.

2. 100 yards interval will be maintained between Platoons and equivalent units.

3. Normal halts at 10 minutes to every hour will be observed.
   Brigade time will be notified between 10 & 11 a.m. this morning.

4. 1st Line Transport will march in rear of Battalion.

5. Advanced Parties of 1. N.C.O per Coy & 1 for Headqrs on bicycles will parade at Battn Hqrs at 10. a.m. and proceed to BECOURT. CHATEAU. where they will meet 2/Lieut J.H. Ross at 1-0 p.m.

6. All blankets and surplus Kits will be taken to Brigade Store at No 154 HIGH STREET by 11-0. a.m.
   Officers Kits going with the Battn will be taken to ~~Brigade~~ Quartermaster's Stores by 1-0. p.m.
   Mess boxes will be collected at 1-30 p.m.

George W. Duncan.
--------------------------- Captain
Adjutant : 8th Battn Seaforth Highlanders

Copy No 1 -- O.C. "A" Coy
     2 -- O.C. "B" Coy
     3 -- O.C. "C" Coy.
     4 -- O.C. "D" Coy.
     5 -- Lewis Gun Officer.
     6 -- Transport Officer.
     7 -- Quartermaster.
     8 -- 2nd in Command.
     9 -- War Diary.
    10 -- File.

Appendix VIII

44th Brigade B.M.31.

O.C. 8th Seaforth Hrs.

The 8th Seaforths will find a working party of 300 O.R. and necessary officers to do road work in relief of the 46th Infantry Brigade as under :-

100 men on LA BOISELLE - CONTALMAISON Road rendezvous X.19.b.0.9. at 8-30 A.M. 6th Instant when they will report to the R.E. officer in charge of roads.

200 men on FRICOURT - CONTALMAISON Road rendezvous X.27.b.1.1. at 8-30 A.M. 6th instant reporting to O.C. "C" Coy. 2nd Labour Battalion.

The party will be bivouaced at BECOURT and proceed daily to the place of work.

If buses can be procured for the working party they will leave here 6-30 A.M. 6th instant. If buses are not procurable they will march to bivouac at BECOURT to-day at 2 P.M.

Definite orders for proceeding will be sent by 11 A.M.

Captain,
Brigade Major,
44th Infantry Brigade.

5-10-16.

"A" Form.

MESSAGES AND SIGNALS.

TO	8th Seaforths 7th Camerons 44th T.M. Battery

Sender's Number.	Day of Month	In reply to Number	
B.M. 60	25		AAA

8th Seaforths will not now provide working party tomorrow AAA Men will march with unit AAA 7th Camerons will now pass Starting Point at original time and T.M. Battery 10 minutes later than shown

From 44th I.B.
Place
Time 10.15 pm

W Gauge Capt B.M.

Appendix X

S E C R E T. Copy No. 2

44th Infantry Brigade Operation Order No.99.

Reference Maps. 8-10-16.
  15th Div.Maps Nos.10 & 10a. d/3-10-16.
  and 57D.S.E.2 and 57C.S.W.1. (parts of).

1. The 44th Infantry Brigade will relieve the 68th Infantry Brigade on the front from the MARTINPUICH – WARLENCOURT Road, exclusive, at about M.22.b.4.7. to M.16.a.2.5. The above map references are subject to variation as the tactical situation may alter.

2. Machine Gun and Trench Mortar Commanders will arrange reliefs direct with their opposite numbers.

   Guides as per relief table – shown on back hereof.

3. The 73rd Field Coy.R.E., less two sections, will come under 44th Infantry Brigade on completion of relief.

4. All movements from bivouacs to be by platoons at 200 yards interval.

5. A party of 1 N.C.O. and 20 men from each battalion – for work in connection with Dumps – will relieve a similar party at M.34.a.8.5. (North of HIGH WOOD).
   Rendezvous at Cemetery on BECOURT – ALBERT Road, 2 P.M.
   The 9th Black Watch will detail a Captain or Lieutenant to command this party.
   The 7th Cameron Hrs. will detail a 2/Lieutenant to assist.
   The Officer in Charge will report to Officer in Charge of party to be relieved at S.3.b.6.0.

6. The 4 companies 8th Seaforth Hrs. at present carrying for 68th and 69th Infantry Brigades move direct to their allotted areas under arrangements made by the 68th Infantry Brigade.

7. Brigade Headquarters will close at 4 P.M. and open simultaneously at M.33.a.1.9.

Issued through
Signals.
1.30 P.M.

Kenneth Barge, Captain,
Brigade Major,
44th Infantry Brigade.

Copies to :-
  1. 9th Black Watch.   2. 8th Seaforths.   3. 9/10th Gordons.
  4. 7th Camerons.   5. 44 M.G.Coy.   6. 44 T.M.Battery.
  7. 15th Div.   8. 69th Inf.Bde.   9. 45th Inf.Bde.
  10. 46th Inf.Bde.   11. 69th Inf.Bde.   12. Left Bde.17th Div.
  13. 15 Div.Arty.   14. III Corps H.A.   15. Bde.Bombing Offcr.
  16. Bde.Signal Offcr. 17. Bde.Transport O. 18. "   Supply Offcr.
  19. Staff Captain.   20. War Diary.   21. File.

Table to accompany 44th Infantry Brigade Operation Order No.99.

Relieving Unit.	Unit being relieved.	Guides, Time & Place.	Remarks.
8th Seaforths H.Qrs.	10th North. Fusrs.	2 guides, CONTALMAISON VILLA, 2 P.M.	By
7th Camerons.	11th North. Fusrs.	1 guide per platoon, 1 for H.Q. CONTALMAISON VILLA 3 P.M.	most
44 M.G.Coy.	68 M.G.Coy.	(Guides CONTALMAISON VILLA. 2-30 P.M.	convenient
44 T.M.Battery.	68 T.M.Bty.	(	route.
9th Black Watch.	13th D.L.I.	Guides, 1 per platoon, 1 per Strong Point, 1 for H.Qrs. CONTALMAISON VILLA. 5-0 P.M.	
8/10th Gordons.	12th D.L.I.	- do - 6-0 P.M.	

Appendix X

44th Brigade B.M.31.

All Battns. 44th Inf.Bde.
73rd Fld.Coy.R.E.

Each battalion will detail 25 O.R. as a permanent carrying party, to work under the 73rd Field Coy.R.E. The 8th Seaforth Hrs. will detail an officer to be in charge of the whole party (100 O.R.).

Each party will march independently to S.13.b.7.4. (between BAZENTIN-le-PETIT and MAMETZ Wood, and can be discerned by green waterproof sheets which cover material) reporting to the H.Q. 73rd Field Coy. R.E. at 8 A.M./0th instant.

Men will carry their 100% tools and their day's rations.   Battalions will arrange for parties to be provided with one dixie each.

Captain,
Brigade Major,
44th Infantry Brigade.

9-10-16.

Appendix XI

SECRET.   Copy No. 2

44th Infantry Brigade Operation Order No.100.
                                              10-10-1916.
                                              XXBXXXXX.

1. Reliefs to be carried out on 10/11th October.
   The 9th Black Watch and 8/10th Gordons will be relieved on the Brigade front by the 7th Cameron Hrs.
   The 8th Seaforth Hrs. will move up into Support.

   On the 11th the Brigade will be disposed as follows :-

   7th Cameron Hrs. 2 Companies in front system.
                     1½ Companies SUNK Road and TANGLE trenches.
                     ½ Company O.G.2.

        Battn. H.Q. M.22.a.4.1. now occupied by 8/10th Gordon Hrs.

   8th Seaforth Hrs. 2 Companies in O.G.1 and between O.G.1.
                     and in advance of PRUE TRENCH.

        Battn. H.Q. CRESCENT ALLEY.

   9th Black Watch. 1 Company PRUE TRENCH.
                     3 Companies in STARFISH LINE.

   8/10th Gordon Hrs. In rear of STARFISH LINE.
        Battn. H.Q. Little BAZENTIN.

2. Relief to be complete by 5 A.M.

3. Battalions will send officers to reconnoitre trenches.

4. All arrangements for relief will be made direct between battalions.

Issued through
  Signals.   Captain,
  2-0 P.M.   Brigade Major,
                                       44th Infantry Brigade.

                Copy No. 1. 9th Black Watch.
                        2. 8th Seaforths.
                        3. 8/10th Gordons.
                        4. 7th Camerons.
                        5. 44 M.G.Coy.
                        6. 44 T.M.Battery.
                        7. 15th Division.
                        8. S.A.Inf.Bde.
                        9. 45th Inf.Bde.
                       10. 15th Div.Arty.
                       11. Liaison Officer.
                       12. 73rd Fld.Coy.R.E.
                       13. Bde.Signal Offcr.
                       14. War Diary.
                       15. File.

Appendix XII

SECRET

Operation Order No 34 — Copy No 6
by Lieut Col N. A. Thomson D.S.O.
Commdg 8th Seaforth Highlanders.
10-10-16

Reference 15 Divn Map No 10 + OB d/3/10/16.

1. The Battn will relieve the 7 Cameron Hrs in Brigade Support tonight as follows:—
   'D' Coy to O.G.1 (about M.21.b and M.22.a.)
   'B' Coy to CRESCENT ALLEY north of PRUE TRENCH
   'A' Coy to PRUE TRENCH
   'C' Coy to PRUE TRENCH.

   Route for 'D' Coy:— CRESCENT ALLEY, SPENCE TRENCH, 26th AVENUE.
   " " 'B', 'A' + 'C' Coys:— CRESCENT ALLEY.

   Battn Hqrs will move to CRESCENT ALLEY about pt M.27.b.9.2
   The hour at which Companies will move off will be notified later.

2. All water bottles will be filled before leaving present position.

3. Cooking in new positions will be under Company arrangement but greatest care must be taken to avoid any smoke as all positions are under close observation.

4. Arrival in new positions to be reported to Battn Hqrs by runner.

                                         Captain
                     Adjt. 8th Battn Seaforth Highlanders

Copy No 1 — OC A Coy.
        2 — OC B Coy.
        3 — OC C Coy.
        4 — OC D Coy.
        5 — L.G.O.
        6 — War Diary
        7 — File.

"C" Form (Original). Army Form C. 2123.
(In books of 50's in duplicate.)
MESSAGES AND SIGNALS. No. of Message............

| Prefix SM | Code AI | Words 56 | Received From AR By WW | Sent, or sent out At ......m. To...... By | Office Stamp. Qr 11/10/16 |

Charges to collect
Service Instructions. AR

Handed in at............................ AR Office 1.45 m. Received 2.5 A.m.

TO   DM attack afforder XIII

| *Sender's Number G 5·90 | Day of Month 11th | In reply to Number — | AAA |

BBB reference from 2 BM 28 of today AAA Operations to commence THREE SIX ONE AAA THREE SIX TWO AAA THREE SIX NOUGHT AAA THREE FIVE FIVE today cancelled AAA These for THREE SIX THREE AAA THREE SIX ONE AAA THREE SIX FIVE AAA THREE FIVE FIVE Hold good AAA Acknowledge

FROM   AR
PLACE & TIME   1·10 P.M.

"C" Form (Duplicate).
MESSAGES AND SIGNALS.

Army Form C. 2123.
(In books of 50's in duplicate.)
No. of Message..............

Service Instructions.

Handed in at.............. Office..........m. Received..........m.

TO: J.B. & D. M, attack appendix XIII

Sender's Number: G.528
Day of Month: 11th
In reply to Number:
AAA

Reference para 5 BM 28 of today for 8.30 pm read 5.30 pm. aaa

FROM: A.R.
PLACE & TIME: 11.25 am

Appendix XIII

S E C R E T.   44th Brigade B.M.28.

All Units 44th Inf.Bde.
    15th Div.   For information.

1.   There will be bombardments of certain objectives on our right to-day and to-morrow 7 A.M. to 5 P.M.

2.   (i) In addition to the above there will be bombardments on whole Corps front at 1-20 P.M. and 3-10 P.M. to-day, 11th instant.
         At 1-40 P.M. and 3-35 P.M. the Left Group Artillery will revert to normal bombardment.
         During these bombardments our trenches will be kept as clear as possible and machine gun fire will be brought to bear on approaches in rear of the enemy trenches.

     (ii). The artillery barrage on enemy trenches opposite the Division will be timed as follows :-
     1-20 P.M. to 1-25 P.M.   Barrage on enemy trenches.
     1-25 P.M. to 1-30 P.M.   Search back by 50 yards
                                     per minute.
     1-30 P.M. to 1-33 P.M.   Jump back to original
                                     objective.
     1-33 P.M. to 1-38 P.M.   Search back by 50 yards
                                     per minute.
     1-38 P.M.   3 salvoes from all batteries
                                     on original objective.
     1-40 P.M.   Resume normal tasks.

         Machine guns will sweep the enemy's parapet at 1-26 P.M. and 1-34 P.M.
         Similar procedure will be followed from 3-15 P.M. to 3-35 P.M.

     (iii). Watches will be synchronised by representatives of units on 11th instant at Brigade Headquarters at 11-30 A.M.

3.   Battalion Observing officers will make special arrangements to note where the enemy places his barrage. Results of this observation to reach Brigade Headquarters not later than 5-30 P.M. 11th instant.

4.   Acknowledge.

                                              Captain,
                                           Brigade Major,
11-10-16.   44th Infantry Brigade.

O.C. A. ⎫
     B. ⎬ Companies
     C. ⎭ &
     D.

SECRET.

The attached Operation Order is forwarded for your information – please initial & pass by bearer.

Companies will stand to arms, ready to move at a moments notice;– 10 minutes before Zero hour –

Zero hour will be notified later.

11/10/16.
10.5 p.m.

George W Duncan.
Capt & Adj
8th Seaforth Highlanders.

10.40 p

"A" Form. Army Form C.2121.
MESSAGES AND SIGNALS. No. of Message...........

Prefix S.M. Code MESS m. | Words 33 | Charge | This message is on a/c of: attack appendices Service XIV | Recd. at........m. Date........ From........ By........
Office of Origin and Service Instructions. AR | Sent At........m. To........ By........ | | (Signature of "Franking Officer.") |

TO DM

Sender's Number.	Day of Month.	In reply to Number.		AAA
*G1539	12			
BBB	reference		AR	ooNo 101
three	three	eight	AA	Three
six	two	AA	Three	six
five	AA	Three	five	five
AA	acknowledge	AA		

From
Place AR
Time 12.15 AM

The above may be forwarded as now corrected. (Z)

Censor. Signature of Addressor or person authorised to telegraph in his name.
* This line should be erased if not required.

S E C R E T.   Copy No. 2

44th Infantry Brigade Operation Order No.101.

11-10-16.

Reference Map.
LE SARS Trench Map.
1/10,000.

1. 9th Division will attack to-morrow at zero. There will be no intense bombardment prior to zero, but the objectives of 9th Division will be bombarded from 5 P.M. October 11th to 7 A.M. October 12th. At zero hour Left Group 15th Divl. Artillery will open intense fire on the trenches in front of Little Wood, and on the Dump at M.16.b, lifting at zero plus 30 minutes.

   The 9th Division advances to its 1st objective at zero, and to its final objective (BUTTE DE WARLENCOURT and trenches in vicinity) at zero plus 20 minutes.

2. (a) 44th Infantry Brigade will co-operate with 1st S.A. Brigade (Left Brigade of 9th Division) by -
   (i) Bringing rifle and machine gun fire to bear on the final objective from 5-30 A.M. to zero on 12th instant.
   (ii) Covering the operations of the 9th Division both during the attack and subsequently by bringing Stokes and Machine Gun fire to bear to the N.E. from about M.16.b.1.3.
   (iii) Advancing on the flank of 9th Division and occupying the enemy dump about M.16.b.6.4.

   (b) The enemy in front of the Brigade will be engaged with rifle, machine gun and trench mortar fire.

   (c) No.4 Special Coy.R.E. will arrange, if wind is favourable, to place a smoke barrage commencing at zero to assist the Division on our right and to cover the front of 15th Div. O.C.7th Cameron Hrs. will assist O.C. No.4 Special Coy.R.E. in every possible way.

3. (i) The capture of the enemy dump will be carried out by 7th Cameron Hrs.

   (ii) The assaulting troops will be formed up in four waves in the trenches in M.16.a. by zero minus 30 minutes. Every precaution must be taken to prevent their being seen prior to the advance.

   (iii) The advance will commence at zero plus 30 minutes (when the barrage will lift) and will be continued to the line M.16.b.9.6. - b.3.5.

   (iv) As soon as this line is reached two strong points will be constructed between the reference points mentioned above. Each of these will be garrisoned by not less than 10 men with a Lewis Gun.
   When darkness permits a trench will be commenced from M.16.b.9.9. to join our present line about M.16.a.8.3., passing through these new strong points.

(2.)

4. 44 L.T.M.Battery at zero will open an intense barrage for two minutes on enemy's trench about Pt.M.16.d.9.9½. Thereafter they will search this trench northwards to quarry at M.17.a.6.0., regulating their fire by the advance of 1st S.A.Brigade.

5. 44 M.G.Company, in addition to co-operating as ordered in para 2 (a) (ii), will arrange to sweep with indirect fire all approaches by which enemy reinforcements might be brought up against 44th and 1st S.A.Brigades.

6. At zero plus 1 hour a contact aeroplane will fly over the line, and advanced infantry will display yellow flares in reply to his signals.

7. Correct time will be distributed to units at Brigade Headquarters four hours before zero.

Zero will be notified later.

Issued through Signals.
8 P.M.

Kenneth Waigg, Captain,
Brigade Major,
44th Infantry Brigade.

Copies to :-
No. 1. 9th Black Watch.
2. 8th Seaforths.
3. 8/10th Gordons.
4. 7th Camerons.
5. 44 M.G.Coy.
6. 44 T.M.Battery.
7. 15th Div.
8. 1st S.A.Bde.
9. 45th Inf.Bde.
10. Left Group Div.Arty.
11. No.4 Special Coy.R.E.
12. Bde.Signalling Offcr.
13. " Bombing Offcr.
14. " Intelligence Offcr.
15. Arty Liaison Offcr.
16. Staff Capt.
17. War Diary.
18. File.

Appendix XVI

SECRET.   Operation Order No 35   Copy No 6
by Lieut Col N.A. Thomson DSO.
Comm'g 6th Batt. Seaforth Highlrs.   12-10-16

1. The Batt. will relieve the 7th Cameron Highrs tonight as follows:-

   "B" Coy will relieve "B" Coy 7th Cameron Hrs in Left firing line.

   "D" Coy will relieve "D" Coy 7th Cameron Hrs in right firing line.

   "C" Coy will relieve "C" Coy 7th Camerons in SUNKEN ROAD and TANGLE TRENCHES.

   "A" Coy will relieve "A" Coy 7th Camerons in O.9.2.

   Companies will move in the above order.

   Route for "B" "C" & "A" Coys:- CRESCENT ALLEY, NEW TRENCH running from CRESCENT ALLEY to FENCE TRENCH, 26th AVENUE.

   Guides, 1 per Platoon from 7th Cameron Hrs will be at junction of 26th AVENUE and O.9.1 at 10.30 p.m.

   Batt. Hqrs will move from present position at 11 p.m. and will open at ~~that hour~~ that hour at 26th AVENUE close to its junction with O.G.1.

2. Companies will not move from present position until rations have arrived, and will report to Batt. Hqrs immediately prior to moving off.

3. One of "A" Coy Lewis Guns will be attached to "B" Coy. One Headquarter Gun will be attached to "D" Coy.

All Trench stores will be taken over, and copies of receipt forwarded to Batta Hqrs, by 9 a.m. 13th inst.

5. Completion of relief will be reported to Batta Hqrs.

George W Dunn Captain
Adjt. 8th Seaforth Hghrs.

Copy No 1 - OC A Coy.
2 - OC B Coy.
3 - OC C Coy.
4 - OC D Coy.
5 - OC 7th Camerons.
6 - War Diary.
7 - File.

Appendix XV

Copy No. 2

S E C R E T.

44th Infantry Brigade Operation Order No.102.

12-10-16.

Reference Map.
LE SARS Trench Map, 1/10,000.

1. 8th Seaforth Hrs. will relieve 7th Cameron Hrs. in front line, commencing 12 MIDNIGHT 12th/13th.

   All details to be arranged between Commanding Officers.

   On completion of relief 7th Cameron Hrs. will occupy the positions vacated by 8th Seaforth Hrs.

2. Completion of relief to be reported to Brigade H.Qrs.

3. Acknowledge.

Issued through
Signals.
12-50 P.M.

Captain,
Brigade Major,
44th Infantry Brigade.

Copies to :-
No. 1. 9th Black Watch.   5. 44 M.G.Coy.   9. 45th Inf.Bde.
    2. 8th Seaforths.   6. 44 T.M.Bty.   10. Bde.Signal.Offcr.
    3. 8/10th Gordons.   7. 15th Div.   11. " Bombing "
    4. 7th Cameron Hrs.   8. 1st S.A.Bde.   12. War Diary.
                                              13. File.

Appendix XVII

Operation Orders by Lieut-Colonel C.H. Marsh, D.SO.   COPY No 1
Commanding 7th (service) Battalion Cameron Highlanders

SECRET   Thursday 12th October 1916.

1. The 7th Cameron Highlanders will be relieved on the night of the 12/13th October by the 8th SEAFORTH HIGHLANDERS.

    "A" Company 7th Cameron Highrs will be relieved by "A" Coy 8th SEAFORTH HRS
    "B"   -do-   -do-   "B"   do.
    "C"   -do-   -do-   "C"   -do-
    "D"   -do-   -do-   "D"   do.

RELIEF

If this afternoon's operations are successful, a tape will be laid out by O.C. "A" Company, 7th Cameron Highlanders along which a trench has to be dug connecting the strong points established by "D" Company, 7th Cameron Highlanders on the SOUTHERN SIDE of the LE SARS – BAPAUME ROAD with the trench presently occupied by "B" Company, 7th Cameron Highlanders on the NORTH side of the road. On the tape being laid out O.C. "A" Company, 7th Cameron Highlanders will send the party which laid the tape to report to O.C. "D" Company 8th Seaforth Highlanders, O.G.1. This party will guide "D" Company, 8th Seaforth Highlanders to take over the strong points held by "D" Company and shew them the location of the tape. On this being done "D" Company, 7th Cameron Highlanders will withdraw to O.G.1 and remain there until the other "B" "C" & "A" Companies of 8th SEAFORTH HIGHLANDERS have passed up. 26th AVENUE

Order of incoming of the other three Companies, 8th Seaforth Hrs
    "B" — "C" — "A"

"A", "B" & "C" Companies, 7th Cameron Highlanders will each provide 4 Guides (1 per platoon) to guide incoming companies of 8th Seaforth Hrs. They will report at Battalion Headquarters at 10.30 P.M.

Receipts will be taken for Trench Stores which will be sent to Battalion Headquarters tomorrow by 10 a.m.

— (CONTINUED) —

Secret   Thursday 12th October 1916

Capt Duncan

If this holds good it means
that our D is liable to
leave O.G. before it
opens its gates—and also
that our working party
from A Coy does
stand with orders as
shown on tape's laid

I Heard that Cameron
please arrange with Babs
D to report to my Bab.
as soon as tape's laid so
that I can send up writing
part of A Coy at once
and (2) that our D or Coy is independ-

OPERATION ORDERS (CONTINUED)

PAGE 2

On relief platoons will move off independently and Companies will occupy the following new positions:-

<u>'A' Company</u> in CRESCENT ALLEY between H.Q Coy and PRUE TRENCH.
<u>'B' Company</u> in PRUE TRENCH – RIGHT.
<u>'C' COMPANY</u> in O.G.1.
<u>'D' COMPANY</u> in PRUE TRENCH – LEFT
<u>BATTALION HEAD QUARTERS</u> in CRESCENT ALLEY.

(Signed) Geo. J. S. Lumsden,
  Lieutenant & A/Adjutant.
7th Cameron Highlanders

Issued at   p.m. To:-

Copy No 1 to O.C. 8th Seaforth Hrs.   Copy No 6 to L.G.O.
   . 2 . O.C. 'A' Company   . 7 . R.S.M.
   . 3 . O.C. 'B' Company   . 8 . War Diary
   . 4 . O.C. 'C' Company   . 9 . File.
   . 5 . O.C. 'D' Company   . 10   Adjutant

working party going up, that
is after they have got their
rations & their (D Coy) guides
to be at 26th Avenue at
10-30 pm

(3) That the Covering party
is to be found by Carrington's
until our D relieve them
D Coy then they
will hand over the covering
arrangements to our
D Coy if the work is not
completed

Appendix XVIII

44th Brigade. B.M. 31.

All Battns. 44th Inf. Bde.
73rd Field Coy. R.E.
15th Division.

Work to be carried out on the night 13/14th Oct.

1. The 8/10th Gordon Highrs. will dig a communication trench from M.16.a.4.5. through orchards to cross roads at M.16.c.1.3½.

2. The 8th Seaforth Highrs. will deepen the trench from Cutting at M.16.c.5.2. to the road at M.16.b.2.2.

   The trench heads on each side of the road about M.16.b.2.2½. will be brought up to within 5 yards of the road and dug to a depth of 2 feet for about 15 yards from the ends; the heads to be brought exactly opposite each other.

3. The 73rd Field Coy. R.E. will make preparations to dig a tunnel under the road joining the two trench heads.

4. Until further orders Battalions will be responsible for work as under (this cancels B.M.31 of 11th instant).

   Front line Battalion.

   Front trenches and 26TH AVENUE as far back as Battn. H.Qrs.

   Support Battn.

   28TH AVENUE and SPHOE Trench as far as junction with CREDIT ALLEY.

   This is in addition to the normal duties of general trench improvements.

13th October 1916.

Captain,
Brigade Major 44th Inf. Bde.

44th Brigade.
B.M. 31.

O. C., 9th Black Watch,
    8th Seaforth Highrs.,
    8/10th Gordon Highrs.,
    73rd Field Coy. R.E.
H.Qrs. 15th Division.
O. C., 7th Cameron Hrs. - for information.

Work to be carried out night 14/15th October in addition to the normal trench improvements.

1. 9th Black Watch will detail 2 Officers and 80 men to dig a trench from M.16.a.5.5. to 5.7.
   The trench will be taped out by R.E.
   They should meet R.E. Officer at 8 p.m. at M.16a.5.5.
   Tools 100%.
   8th Seaforth Hrs. will supply covering party.

2. 8/10th Gordon Hrs. will detail 4 Officers and 200 Other Ranks to complete Communication Trench from M.16.c.5.9. to about M.16.a.7.4.
   Site will be taped out by 8th Seaforth Hrs.
   Officer in charge with party will meet 4 guides from 8th Seaforths at their H.Qrs. M.22.c.0.8.
   Tools 100%.

   8/10th Gordon Hrs. *with the same party* will also complete the Communication Trench from M.16.c.1.4. to M.16.c.5.9. to standard breadth and depth.

3. 8th Seaforth Highrs will detail 20 men with picks and shovels to assist R.E. at 7 p.m. for work in connection with tunnel under the road at M.16.b.2.2½.

   It is necessary that the 8th Seaforths should deepen the trench leading to tunnel from about M.16.d.1.9. in order that material may be brought up without being seen.

                                              Captain,
                                          Brigade Major,
14th October 1916.   44th Infantry Brigade.

War Diary. *Appendix XX*

SECRET. 15th Div. 100/11 G.a.

44th Inf.Bde.

1. After considering the recommendations of the 44th and 45th Infantry Brigades with regard to the consolidation of the line, the G.O.C. has decided on the following, in addition to the ordinary upkeep of the trenches, as the more urgent work to be carried out by the 46th Inf.Bde. while holding the line :-

(a) To improve and complete existing trenches especially where shown in blue. Fire-stepping is particularly urgent.

(b) To place machine guns in concealed positions (not in front line) where they can bring fire to bear across and beyond the front of the Division.
Supporting machine guns are also necessary.

(c) To dig a new trench facing N.W. near the CHALK PIT as shown in blue.

(d) To place a line of strong points at least 100 yards in front of the front line. The strong points to be approximately parallel with the WARLENCOURT LINE and to be connected up later with the front line and with each other. They are to be taped out by the R.E.

While the above work is mainly in preparation for a further advance, it is particularly important in view of the possibility that we may have to occupy our present line for some days longer, that its defences should be improved.

2. The Divisional Commander also wishes the trench shown in red in M.15.d and b to be dug.
For this work the 44th and 45th Inf.Bdes will, on alternate nights, place working parties of 200 men at the disposal of the 46th Infantry Brigade. They will work under R.E. supervision. The first party will be found by the 45th Infantry Brigade on the night 16/17th October.

3. On the night 16/17th, the 9th Gordon Hrs. under the orders of the C.R.E. will dig a communication trench from GUNPIT TRENCH in M.32.a. to connect with GILBERT ALLEY.

(Sd) H. KNOX, Lieut.Col.,
16-10-16. General Staff, 15th Division.

(2.) 44th Brigade
All Battns. 44th.Inf.Bde. B.M.31.

For information.

The 9th Black Watch will provide the party from this brigade referred to in para 2 above. Details will be intimated later.

Captain,
Brigade Major,
44th Infantry Brigade.
16-10-16.

Maps will follow

SECRET.   Copy No. 2

44th Infantry Brigade Operation Order No.104.
                                                       18-10-16.

Reference Map.-
    15th Div.Maps.Nos.10 & 10a.d/3-10-16.
    and 57d S.E.2 and 57C.S.W.1 (parts of).

1. The 44th Infantry Brigade will relieve the 46th Infantry
    Brigade in the right section front area on the 18th/19th
    and 19th/20th, in accordance with Table shown on reverse.
    Front from WARLENCOURT - FAUCOURT Road to road at M.16.a.2.7.

2. The 73rd Field Coy.R.E. (less 2 sections) will come under
    44th Infantry Brigade on completion of relief.

3. All movements from bivouacs to be by platoons at 200 yards
    interval.

4. Troops will carry 100% tools.

5. The 8th Seaforth Hrs. will leave a guard of 1 N.C.O. and
    3 men in their present Battalion H.Qrs at M.33.a.1.9. until
    further orders.

6. On the 18th October the 10th Sco: Rifles will send an
    advanced party to SCOTS REDOUBT at 2 P.M. to take over
    from the 9th Black Watch.

    On the 19th October the 12th H.L.I. will send an advanced
    party to CUTTING, CONTALMAISON at 2 P.M. to take over
    from the 7th Cameron Hrs.

7. Brigade Headquarters will close at VILLA WOOD at 5 P.M.
    and open simultaneously at M.33.a.1.9.

                                              Captain,
Issued through   Brigade Major,
  Signals.   44th Infantry Brigade.
  1245 M.

        Copies to :-
            No. 1. 9th Black Watch.
                2. 8th Seaforths.
                3. 8/10th Gordons.
                4. 7th Camerons.
                5. 44 M.G.Coy.
                6. 44 T.M.Battery.
                7. 15th Div.
                8. 45th Inf.Bde.
                9. 46th Inf.Bde.
               10. 1st S.A.Bde.
               11. 73rd Fld.Coy.R.E.
               12. 15th Div.Arty.
               13. III Corps H.A.
               14. 45th Fld.Amb.
               15. Bde.Transport Offcr.   19. Bde.Supply Offcr.
               16. " Signal Offcr.   20. Staff Captain.
               17. " Bombing Offcr.   21. War Diary.
               18. No.2 Coy. Train.   22. File.

TABLE TO ACCOMPANY 44TH INFANTRY BRIGADE OPERATION ORDER No.104, dated 18th October, 1916.

18th/19th October.

Relieving Units.	Unit being relieved.	Guides. Time and place.	Route.	Destination.
8/10th Gordon Hrs.	10th Sco: Rifles.	1 per platoon, 1 H.Q. 6 P.M. Junction PRUE TRENCH and CRESCENT ALLEY.	Most convenient.	1 Coy. O.G.1. 1 Coy. CRESCENT ALLEY. 2 Co's PRUE TRENCH. H.Q. CRESCENT - M.27.d.6.6.
8th Seaforth Hrs.	8/10th Gordons.	1 per platoon, 1 H.Q. 5 P.M. Place to be arranged between units.	- do -	2 Co's. SWANSEA TRENCH. 1 Coy. O.G.2. 1 Coy. GOURLAY TRENCH. H.Q. N.W.Corner of BAZENTIN-le-PETIT.
9th Black Watch.	8th Seaforth Hrs.	Not pass O.G.1 before 6 P.M.	- do -	2 Co's STARFISH TRENCH. 1½ Co's. TANGLE. ½ Coy. TYNE STREET. M.33.d.4.4.

19th/20th October.

Relieving Units.	Unit being relieved.	Guides. Time and place.	Route.	Destination.
8/10th Gordons.	12th H.L.I.	1 per platoon, 1 H.Q. 6 P.M. Junction WILLIAM ALLEY and O.G.1.	WILLIAM ALLEY.	Front line system.
9th B.Watch.	8/10th Gordons.	1 per Coy.(1 per platoon for Coy. in O.G.1.) 1 H.Q. 5-45 P.M. Junction PRUE TRENCH and CRESCENT ALLEY.	Most convenient.	1 Coy. O.G.1. 1 Coy. CRESCENT ALLEY. 2 Co's. PRUE. H.Q. CRESCENT ALLEY M.27.d.6.6.
7th Camerons.	9th Black Watch.	1 per platoon, 1 H.Q. 4-45 P.M. CONTALMAISON VILLA.	- do -	2 Co's. STARFISH LINE. 1½ Co's. TANGLE. (H.Q. ½ Coy. TYNE STREET. (M.33.d.4.4.
44 M.G.Coy. 44 T.M.Battery.	46 M.G.Coy. 46 T.M.Battery.	Reliefs to be arranged direct between O.C.Units concerned.		

SECRET.

attach appendix
XXI

ALL UNITS 44th Inf. Bde.   44th Brigade B.M.455.

WARNING ORDER.

The following moves will take place to-day.—

Relieving Units.	Unit being relieved.	Guides. Time and place.	Route.
6/10th Gordon Hrs.	Support Battn. 46th Inf. Bde.	1 per platoon, 1 H.Q. 6 P.M. Junction PRUE TRENCH and CRESCENT ALLEY.	Most convenient.
8th Seaforth Hrs.	8/10th Gordons.	1 per platoon, 1 H.Q. 5 P.M. Place to be arranged between units.	- do -
9th Black Watch.	8th Seaforth Hrs.	Not pass O.G.1. before 6 P.M.	- do -

18-10-16.

W Sarge.
Captain,
Brigade Major,
44th Infantry Brigade.

Secret   Operation Order No 36.   Appendix XXII
          Lieut. Col. N. U. Thomson D.S.O.   Copy No 10
          Commdg: 8th Battn Seaforth Highlanders
                                         18 October 1916.

1. The Battalion will relieve the 8/10th Gordon Highrs tonight as follows:—
     2 Coys in SWANSEA TRENCH
     1 Coy in GOURLEY TRENCH.
     1 Coy in O.G. II.
Battn Headquarters will proceed at 6 p.m. to the Headquarters lately occupied by the 8/10th Gordon Highrs at the N.W. Corner of BAZENTIN LE PETIT WOOD.

2. Companies will move by Platoons commencing at 5-30 p.m. in the following order:—
"A", "B", "D", "C" and will be led by their own guides who have already reconnoitred the ground. — ROUTE — CRESCENT ALLEY.

3. Trench Stores will be taken over and copies of receipts forwarded to Battn Hqrs by 9. a.m. 19th inst.

4. The 9th Battn The Black Watch who are taking over from this Battalion will take up positions as follows:—
     2 Coys in STARFISH TRENCH.
     1½ Coys in TANGLE TRENCH.
     ½ Coy in TYNE TRENCH.
Guides will proceed to CONTALMAISON VILLA to meet The Black Watch at 5-45 p.m and will guide as follows:—
     2 guides from "A" Coy will guide to TYNE TRENCH.
     4 guides from "B" Coy will guide to STARFISH TRENCH.
     4 guides from "D" Coy will guide to STARFISH TRENCH.

5. Completion of relief will be reported to Battn Hqrs.

     ISSUED THROUGH SIGNALS at 4-45 p.m.

                                   G. Blackwood Lieut
                         a/Adjt. 8th Battn Seaforth Highlanders.

Copy No 1 – O.C. "A" Coy   Copy No 6 – Quartermaster.
        2 – O.C. "B" Coy   7 – O/c 8/10th Gordon Hrs.
        3 – O.C. "C" Coy   8 – O/c 9th Black Watch
        4 – O.C. "D" Coy   9 – War Diary.
        5 – Transport Officer.   10 – File.

Appendix XXIII

SECRET.   Copy No. 2

44th Infantry Brigade Operation Order No.105.

21-10-16.

1. The 7th Cameron Hrs. will relieve the 8/10th Gordon Hrs. in the front line to-day, 21st October.

   Owing to the number of working parties out, the relief of the two front companies must be completed between the hours of 7-30 P.M. and 11-30 P.M.

2. The 8th Seaforth Hrs. will move up into 2nd Support and take over area now occupied by the 7th Cameron Hrs.

   The 8th Seaforth Hrs. not to move before 4-45 P.M.

3. All arrangements will be made direct between Officers Commanding concerned.

4. Owing to the state of the trenches, wherever possible movements should be made over the open.

5. Reliefs must be carried out in silence.

6. Report completion by wire.

Issued through
  Signals.
  12 NOON.

                                           Captain,
                                        Brigade Major,
                                     44th Infantry Brigade.

        Copies to :-

              No. 1. 9th Black Watch.
                 2. 8th Seaforths.
                 3. 8/10th Gordons.
                 4. 7th Camerons.
                 5. 44 M.G.Coy.
                 6. 44 T.M.Battery.
                 7. 15th Div.
                 8. 45th Inf.Bde.
                 9. 27th Inf.Bde.
                10. 15th Div.Arty.
                11. Bde.Signal Offcr.
                12. Bde.Bombing Offcr.
                13. Bde.Transport Offcr.
                14. Staff Capt.
                15. War Diary.
                16. File.

Appendix XXIV

44th Brigade B.M.51.

9th Gordon Hrs. (Pioneers).
All Battns. 44th Inf.Bde.
73rd Fld.Coy.R.E.
H.Q.15th Division. }
45th Inf.Bde.   } For information.

The following work will be carried out to-day, in addition to the normal trench improvements.

1. **8th Seaforth Hrs.**   4 officers and 200 men.

    (a) To improve and fire-step the jumping-off trench from M.16.b.3.6. to M.10.c.8.¼.

    (b) Produce the jumping-off trench from M.16.b.3.6. through CUTTING ROAD to BAPAUME ROAD at M.16.b.Cent:

    (c) Produce the jumping-off trench from M.10.c.8.¼. due east for a distance of 100 yards, or to junction with 45th Inf.Bde. if not so far.
    Both extensions to be fire-stepped and dug to a depth of 4-feet.   Site will be taped out by R.E.

    Route over the open close to JOCK ALLEY.
    No guides.   Tools 100%.
    Work to commence at 7 P.M.

2. **7th Cameron Hrs.**

    (a) To dig a trench from M.16.b.2.2. (20 yards from Tunnel entrance) to the road junction at M.16.b.8¾.½. (a line through a derelict locomotive gives the right direction).
    R.E. will tape out site.

    (b) Broaden LE SARS TRENCH SOUTH from about M.16.c.7.3. to M.16.d.5.5.

3. **9th Black Watch.**   2 officers and 75 men.

    Dig an assembly trench from Coy.H.Q.at M.16.a.8.1. close under the hedge on the Southern side as far as JOCK ALLEY.
    Advanced party will mark out site.
    Work to commence at 7 P.M.   Tools 100%.

4. (a) The 73rd Field Coy.instead of making a tunnel under the road at M.16.b.2.2½. will dig and complete a trench 8-ft.deep - 3-ft.6-in broad at the top and 18 inches at the bottom. - Top of this trench to be blinded.

    (b) Will have the sites in para 1 (b) and (c) and 2(a) taped out by 7 P.M.

5. 9th Gordon Hrs.(Pioneers) will dig a boyau from the front line at M.16.a.4½.5. to the nearest point in the newly dug jumping-off trench in front.

6. 7th Cameron Hrs. will furnish all covering parties for work being carried out to-night.

                                      Captain,
                                      Brigade Major,
22-10-16.   44th Infantry Brigade.

P.S.

9th Black Watch will dig a trench from M.16.d.4.8. to M.16.d.7.7. where they will join up with a post established by the 9th Division on our right.

Trench to be standard depth, breadth, and will be waved.

An officer from 7th Cameron Hrs. will reconnoitre and tape out site. Officer in charge 9th Black Watch party to meet this officer at M.16.d.4.8. at 7 P.M.

Tools 100%.

Route - close proximity to LE SARS TRENCH SOUTH.

P.T.O.

Appendix XXV
Copy No. 2

SECRET

Work. 44th Inf Bde.

The following working parties will be detailed tonight –

1. 8th Seaforth Highlanders 4 officers and 200 men
   (a) To dig jumping off trench from M16 B 6.5½ to 16 B 1½ 6
   (b) To improve and fire step SCOTLAND TRENCH.
   (c) To carry on extension towards 45th Bde (westwards) 80 yards.
   The site for (a) will be taped out by R.E.
   Route over the open between LESARS SOUTH TRENCH & LE SARS.
   No guides — Tools 100%.
   Work to commence at midnight —

2. The 7th Cameron Highlanders will leave sufficient officers and men to complete a trench from M 16 B 2 2 (20 yards from Tunnel entrance) to road junction at M16 B 8¾.½ (a line thro' derelict locomotive)
   The 7th Camerons will tape out the site.
   Trench to be completed by 4 am.

3. The 9th Black Watch will dig a trench from Post at M 16 D 5½ 6½ to join up with post of 9th Division at M16 D 7 7.
   Work to commence after relief —
   9th B.W. will tape out site — Tools 100%.
   Trench to be completed by 4 am.

4. The 8/10th Gordons will deepen and widen LE SARS TRENCH SOUTH from M16 C 8 4 thro M16 D 2 6. to M16 D 3 9½.
   2 officers 100 men.
   No guides. Tools 100%.
   Work to commence at midnight.

5. Tape will be sent to 9th B.W. and 7th Camerons on the afternoon of the 23rd.

6. Immediately a trench has been begun throughout, the officer in charge of the party must see the tape is rolled up and returned to Battn. H.Q.

7. All Trenches must be dug to standard depth and breadth.

Copies to (1) 9th B.W. (2) 8th Seaforths (3) 8/10th Gordons.
(4) 7th Camerons. (5) 3rd Field Coy. R.E.

Kenneth Sarge Capt.
Brigade Major 44th Inf. Bde.

Issued thro' Sigs
1.30 pm
23.10.16

S.T. Operation Order No 58 Appendix XXVI
       Copy No 5

Lieut Col. H.A. Thomson D.S.O.
And 8th Seaforth Highrs.

24th Oct 1916

Battn will relieve the 9th Black Watch in
front system tonight in the following order:-
A Coy relieves B Coy 9th B.W. in left firing line
C Coy   "   D Coy   "   " in Right "   "
D Coy   "   "A" Coy "   " " Support
B Coy   "   "C" Coy "   " " Reserve.

Guides from 9th B.W. (1 per platoon & 1 per H.Qrs) will be
at junction SPENCE TRENCH & WILLIAM ALLEY (new
trench which joins CRESCENT ALLEY with SPENCE
TRENCH). at 6.30 pm.

2. Greatcoats will be carried - all water bottles
will be filled & as much water as possible
carried up in petrol tins -

3. Battn HQrs will close at present position at 8.30pm
& open at the same time in 26th Avenue (M.2.d.9.8)

4. Lewis Gun Officer will detail 1 L.G. to proceed
with A Coy & 1 L.G. with "C" Coy. These are in
addition to the Company guns -

5. Completion of relief to be reported by wire to
Battn HQrs.

George W Duncan
Capt & Adjt
8/Seaforth Highrs

No 1. OC A Coy
   2 OC B Coy
   3 OC C Coy
   4 OC D Coy
   5 HQ Diary
   6 File.

Appendix XXVII

SECRET.   Copy No. 2

44th Infantry Brigade Operation Order No.108.

24-10-16.

1. The following reliefs and moves will take place on the 24/25th October in accordance with Brigade Operation Order No.106 dated 23rd October, 1916.

2. The 8/10th Gordon Hrs. will relieve the 9th Black Watch in the right front system. The part of the 9th Black Watch relieved will move into their battalion area.

   Relief to be completed by 9 P.M.

3. The 7th Cameron Hrs. and 8th Seaforth Hrs. will not commence to move forward to their respective areas before 9 P.M.

4. 44 M.G.Coy., and 44 L.T.M.Battery will conform to the above.

5. (i) All troops to be in position by 5 A.M. 25-10-16.

   (ii) The importance of silence during the relief must be impressed on all ranks. Once troops are in position movement must be reduced to a minimum.

6. Arrangements for relief will be made direct between the Officers Commanding concerned.

7. Completion of relief to be reported by wire to Brigade Headquarters at M.27.c.3.½.

Issued through
Signals.
8 A.M.

Kenneth Barge
Captain,
Brigade Major,
44th Infantry Brigade.

Copies to :-

No. 1. 9th Black Watch.
    2. 8th Seaforth Hrs.
    3. 8/10th Gordons.
    4. 7th Cameron Hrs.
    5. 44 M.G.Coy.
    6. 44 T.M.Battery.
    7. 15th Division.
    8. 15th Div.Arty.
    9. 45th Inf.Bde.
    10. 27th Inf.Bde.
    11. Bde.Signal Offcr.
    12. " Bombing Offcr.
    13. 73rd Fld.Coy.R.E.
    14. Staff Capt.
    15. War Diary.
    16. File.

44th Brigade B.M.31.

SECRET.

WORK. 44th Infantry Brigade.

O.C. 8th Seaforths.
8/10th Gordons.
7th Camerons.
73rd Fld.Coy.R.E.
9th Black Watch. For information.

The following working parties will be detailed to-night.-

1. **8th Seaforth Hrs.**
   To complete work detailed in work orders of 23rd instant, less the boyau extension.
   Detailed instructions with reference to extension of SCOTLAND TRENCH east will be given verbally to officer in charge of that party who will report to Brigade H.Qrs.

2. **7th Cameron Hrs.** 2 Officers and 100 men.
   Broaden and deepen LE SARS TRENCH SOUTH from
              M.16.c.9.5. through M.16.d.2.6. to M.16.d.3.½.
   Work to commence at 1 A.M. 25th instant.
   Guides Nil.   Tools 100%.   Route - most convenient.

3. **8/10th Gordon Hrs.** 1 Officer and 50 men.
   Will extend left boyau from 16.a.4⅜.8. to 16.a.4½.9½.
   Site is already taped.   Guides nil.
   Work to commence at 7-30 P.M.   Tools 100%.
   Route through the orchard by JOCK ALLEY.

4. Unless trenches are commenced at a proper breadth it is little better than wasted labour.

5. An officer or N.C.O. from the 73rd Field Coy.R.E. will meet officer in charge of working party for SCOTLAND TRENCH east extension at trench head at 7-30 P.M.

Captain,
Brigade Major,
44th Infantry Brigade.

24-10-16.

Right Part   25 ~~24~~ Workers
              10 ~~10~~ Covering

Left Part   20 Workers
              10 Covering

Centre Improvement) 25 Workers
Party   )

$$\frac{65}{25} \over 88$$

~~=~~ 90
===

Right Part — 25 Workers $\overline{90\text{ yds}}$
             10 Covering

Left Part $\overline{80\text{ yds}}$
             20 Workers
             8 Covering

Span = 150" = 12' = 4 yds

4)90   4)80
  25   20

44th Brigade B.M.29/1.

15th Division 114/3.A.A.

S E C R E T.

44th Inf.Bde.

Right Sector III Corps during to-day and on night of 24th/25th.

150th Infantry Brigade will be on the left of the 50th Division.

The G.O.C. 50th Division assumes command of the Right Sector at 9 A.M. on the 25th instant.

(Sd) H. KNOX, Lieut.Col.,
General Staff, 15th Division.

24-10-16.

(2.)

All Units 44th Inf.Bde.

For information.

Mack
Captain,
Brigade Major,
44th Infantry Brigade.

24-10-16.

Appendix XXIX

UNITS.	OCTOBER.					
	24/25.	25/26	26/27	27/28	28/29	29/30
9th Black Watch.	SCOTS REDOUBT. D.	SCOTS REDOUBT. D.	SCOTS REDOUBT. D.	A. H.Q. M.16.c.		
9/10th Gordons.	BAZENTIN.	BAZENTIN.	BAZENTIN.	A. H.Q. M.16.c.		
7th Camerons.	CUTTING.	CUTTING.	CUTTING.	" M.22.a.4.1.		
8th Seaforths.	A	A	B	" M.21.d.9½.8½ d.		
10th Scot:Rifles.	C	C	C	1st Reserve. HQ.M.27.d.5.4.		
12th H.L.I.	B	B	A	2nd Reserve. HQ.M.33.d.5.4.		

LIABLE TO ALTERATION.

S E C R E T.
44th Infantry Brigade Operation Order No. 111.
Copy No.

25-10-18.

1. The 12th H.L.I. will relieve the 8th Seaforth Hrs. in the front line system to-day 26th October. On the relief the 8th Seaforth Hrs will move into the area vacated by the 12th H.L.I.

2. Relief will commence at dusk.

3. All arrangements will be made between officers commanding.

4. Completion of relief to be reported by wire to Bde.H.Q.

Issued through
Signals.
11-15 A.M.

W. Waugh Captain,
Brigade Major,
44th Infantry Brigade.

No. 1. 9th Black Watch.
2. 8th Seaforth Hrs.
3. 8/10th Gordon Hrs.
4. 7th Cameron Hrs.
5. 44 M.G.Coy.
6. 44 M.G.Coy. T M Bty
7. 15th Div.
8. 12th H.L.I.
9. 10th Scot Rifles.
10. 46th Inf.Bde.
11. 45th Inf.Bde.
12. /50 th Inf.Bde.
13. 73rd.Fld.Coy.R.E.
14. Staff Capt.
15. War Diary.
16. File.

SECRET — Operation Order No 39 appendix XXXI
Copy No. 7
by Lt Col N.A. Thomson DSO
Cmdg 5/Seaforth Highrs
26th Oct 1916

1. The Battalion will be relieved tonight by 12th H.L.I tonight in the following order:—
"A" Coy will be relieved by "A" Coy 12th H.L.I
"C" Coy "   "   "   " "C" "   "   "   "   "
"D" Coy "   "   "   " "D" "   "   "   "   "
"B" Coy "   "   "   " "B" "   "   "   "   "

Guides (1 per platoon) from "A" Coy 8th Sea Highrs will be at H.Q. "A" Coy 12th H.L.I. O.G.1. at 5.45 p.m.
Guides (1 per platoon) from "B" "C" & "D" Coys 8th Sea Highrs will be at junction of WILLIAM ALLEY & SPENCE TRENCH at 5.45 p.m.
Route — over the open.

2. On relief Companies of 8th Sea Highrs will move as follows:—
"A" & "C" Coys to PRUE TRENCH — "A" on the left & "C" on the right
"B" Coy to CRESCENT ALLEY
"D" Coy to O.G.I

Companies will each send one officer & 1 N.C.O. at 2 p.m. today to take over the line from 12th H.L.I.

3. Advance parties of 1 N.C.O. per Coy from 12th H.L.I will arrive at 2 p.m. today to take over trench stores. Receipts will be forwarded to Battn HQrs by 9 a.m. 27th inst.

4. Battn HQrs will close in present position on completion of relief & will move to CRESCENT ALLEY H.N.27.d.5.4.

2

5. On completion of relief "A" & "C" Coys will each return 1 L.G. & team to Batt. H.Qrs.

6. Completion of relief to be reported by wire to Batt. H.Qrs.
Companies will also report when they have taken up their new positions.

Issued thro' Sigs at ——

George W. Duncan
—————————— Captain
Adjutant 8th Seaforth Highrs.

Copy No 1.   OC "A" Coy
     2   B
     3   C
     4   D
     5   OC 12th H.L.I.
     6.   War Diary
     7.   File.

Appendix XXXII

SECRET.   44th Brigade B.M.32.

O.C. 8th Seaforth Hrs.
     12th H.L.I.,
     10th Scot Rifles.
     15th Division. For information.

The following working parties will be detailed to-night.-

1. **8th Seaforth Hrs.**
   With the necessary number of men available in the front line system will dig a jumping-off trench 4-ft deep, 3-ft.6 broad at top and 1-ft.6 at bottom from M.16.b.2½.6. through the SUNK Road to the BAPAUME Road at M.16.b.5.5.
   The site has been already taped out by the R.E. Work to commence at 6 P.M.

2. **12th H.L.I.**
   (a) Will deepen and broaden northern end of BOYAU from M.16.a.3.7. to the junction of SCOTLAND TRENCH.

   (b) Deepen, improve and fire-step SCOTLAND TRENCH where necessary.

3. **10th Sco:Rifles.**
   (a) 2 officers and 60 men will remove mud from, and improve JOCK ALLEY.   Tools 100% shovels.

   (b) 2 officers and 80 men will remove mud from, and improve LE SARS SOUTH TRENCH from about M.16.c.8.4. to BAPAUME Road M.16.b.2.2. (only inner loop).
   Tools 100% shovels.
Work to commence at midnight.
This work to be done must be reconnoitred through the day.
     No guides.   Route - most convenient.

                                        Captain,
                                   for Brigade Major,
                                   44th Infantry Brigade.

26-10-16.

O.C. A.
B. } Companies
D.

Appendix XXXII
A/13/26.

1. Following party of 2 off & 100 men will be found tonight as follows:—
   "B" Coy - 1 off & 60 men.
   "D" Coy - 1 off & 40 men.

   Work. Dig a jumping off trench 4ft deep, 3ft 6 wide at top & 1ft 6in at bottom from M.16.b.2½.6 through the sunk Road to the BAPAUME ROAD at M.16.b.5.5. Site has been taped out by R.E.

2. Party will rendez-vous at "D" Coy HQrs. at 6.15 p.m.

3. Covering party of 1 off & 12 men will be found by "A" Coy & will be at junction of LE SARS TRENCH NORTH & BAPAUME ROAD at 6.45 p.m.

4. Party will be under CAPT A.W. TURNBULL.

5. On completion of work party will rejoin their respective Coys in new position.

6. Acknowledge —

26/10/16.
3.30 p.m.

George W Duncan.
Capt. & Adj.
8th Seaforth Highrs.

SECRET   COPY NO. 19

Appendix XXXIV

46th INFANTRY BRIGADE ORDER NO 115

Reference Sheet   28-10-16.
57 c. S.W.

1. Operations have been postponed until 1st November.

2. 46th Infantry Brigade Order No 114 of 27-10-16 is cancelled.

3. Battalions of the 46th Infantry Brigade will remain under the command of G.O.C's 44th and 45th Infantry Brigades for a further period of 48 hours (i.e.) till after relief on October 30/31st.

4. 10th Sco.Rif. will relieve 12th High.L.I. in front line to-day.
This Battalion will not cross POZIERES - HIGH WOOD Crest before 5 p.m. An advanced party will be sent by day to take over Trench Stores. Platoon Guides and Headquarter Guides will be at junction of PRUE Trench and CRESCENT ALLEY at 5.30 p.m.

5. 8th Seaforths will take over CONTALMAISON area from 10th Sco.Rif. All blankets and camp equipment to be handed over and receipts obtained. 8th Seaforths are sending an advanced party to take over at 11 a.m.

6. On completion of relief 10th Sco.Rif. will come under command of 44th Inf.Bde and 8th Seaforths under 46th Inf.Bde.

7. Completion of relief will be reported to Brigade Headquarters.

                                                                                                  Captain,
                                                                                           Brigade Major,
                                                                                   46th Inf. Bde.

Issued at 8.30 a.m.
through Signals

Copy No			
1	War Diary	12.	Bde Transport Officer
2	File	13	No 4 Coy. Train
3	7/8th K.O.S.B.	14	15th Division.
4	10th Sco.Rif.	15	44th Inf.Bde
5	10/11th High.L.I.	16	45th Inf.Bde.
6	12th High.L.I.	17	6/7th R.Sc.Fus.
7	46th M.G.Coy.	18	9th Black Watch
8	46th T.M.Bty.	19	8th Seaforths
9	Staff Captain	20	11th Argl & Suth'd H.
10	Bde Supply Officer	21	A.P.M., 15th Division
11	Bde Signal Officer		

TRENCH MAP, 4th ARMY FRONT. MAP D. 25-10-16.
Trenches corrected to 24-10-16.

Appendix XXXVI

Appendix XXXVI

CONFIDENTIAL

WAR DIARY

of

8th (Service) Battalion Seaforth Highlanders.

From 1st Nov. 1916 To 30th Nov. 1916

(Volume IV)

In the Field.
30/11/1916.

..........................Lt Colonel.
Comdg; 8th (Ser) Battalion Seaforth Highlanders.

WAR DIARY or INTELLIGENCE SUMMARY

Army Form C. 2118.

Place	Date	Hour	Summary of Events and Information	Remarks and references to Appendices
CONTALMAISON	1/4/16		Working party of 250 on roads in vicinity of CONTALMAISON. Battalion under Lt Col 46th Inf Bgde. In accordance with 46th Inf Bgde O.O. no 119 the Bn moved to BECOURT. Relief reported complete at 11 P.M.* Battalion rested to 44th Bgde on completion of relief. CONTALMAISON HQRs taken over by Bn inventories — *Report much delayed owing to confusion about billet arrangements at BECOURT Casualties Wounded O.R. 1.	Appendix I Appendix II B4B
BECOURT	2/4/16		Working party of 300 or as supplied for work on FRICOURT — CONTALMAISON road. Reported to & worked under O.C. "C" Coy. 2nd Labour Btn.	Appendix III B4B
BECOURT	3/4/16		Working party of 300 or as on 2nd inst.	B4B
BECOURT	4/4/16		Working party of 100 on work in Camp under direction of the Town Major. Bn had use of Divisional Baths at BECOURT from 3 pm. to 4 pm. Casualties Wounded O.R. 1	Appendix IV B4B

WAR DIARY
or
INTELLIGENCE SUMMARY.
(Erase heading not required.)

Army Form C. 2118.

Place	Date	Hour	Summary of Events and Information	Remarks and references to Appendices
BECOURT	5/11/16		The Battn. moved to BRESLE in accordance with Bgde O.O. 119 and Bttn O.O. 43. Bttn. arrived in billets at 3.30 p.m. GYN	Appendix V -do- VI
BRESLE	6/11/16		The Bttn was employed on kit inspections & general cleaning up under Coy arrangements. At about 10.30 P.M. loud explosions were heard. These came from a fire evidently at an ammunition dump having a true bearing of 14°. The sound of the explosions took 26 seconds to travel. Wind moderate about due south. Explosions continued throughout the night. Requisitions put in for material for improvement of billets. GYN	Appendix VII
BRESLE	7/11/16		Very wet weather rendered outside training impossible. Bttn again employed under Coy. was general cleaning up, kit inspections etc. GYN	Appendix VII

Army Form C. 2118.

WAR DIARY
or
INTELLIGENCE SUMMARY.
(Erase heading not required.)

Instructions regarding War Diaries and Intelligence Summaries are contained in F. S. Regs., Part II. and the Staff Manual respectively. Title pages will be prepared in manuscript.

Place	Date	Hour	Summary of Events and Information	Remarks and references to Appendices
BRESLE	8/11/16		Training as per programme.	Appendix VII
BRESLE	9/11/16		Training as per programme. S.O. C-in-C. inspected the Bln. on the training ground.	Appendix VIII
BRESLE	10/11/16		Training as per programme. Considerable enemy aerial activity during the night & several bombs dropped in vicinity of BRESLE	Appendix VII
BRESLE	11/11/16		Bln. duty Bn. Working parties of 150 or work in roads etc in BRESLE & vicinity. Remainder of Bn. platoon & other drill under Coy arrangements. Route march cancelled.	
BRESLE	12/11/16		In the forenoon Church Parade. Inspection of Billets by the C.O.	Appendix IX

T/2134. Wt. W708—776. 500000. 4/15. Sir J. C. & B.

WAR DIARY
or
INTELLIGENCE SUMMARY.
(Erase heading not required.)

Army Form C. 2118.

Place	Date	Hour	Summary of Events and Information	Remarks and references to Appendices
BRESLE	13/10/16		Bn. Route March at 9.30 A.M. Route BRESLE, BAIZIEUX, FRANVILLERS, HEILLY, RIBEMONT, BRESLE.	Appendix IX
BRESLE	14/10/16		Training as per programme. Riding school for junior officers	JJB
BRESLE	15/10/16		Bn. employed entirely on watching parties under direction of the town mayor	JJB
BRESLE	16/10/16		Training as per programme	JJB
BRESLE	17/10/16		Training as per programme	JJB
BRESLE	18/10/16		Inclement weather rendered training out of doors impossible. Lectures in billets under Coy. arrangements. In the forenoon working party of 1 officer & 40 or dismissed by town mayor on account of weather conditions	JJB

Army Form C. 2118.

WAR DIARY
or
INTELLIGENCE SUMMARY.
(Erase heading not required.)

Instructions regarding War Diaries and Intelligence Summaries are contained in F. S. Regs., Part II. and the Staff Manual respectively. Title pages will be prepared in manuscript.

Place	Date	Hour	Summary of Events and Information	Remarks and references to Appendices
BRESLE	19/11/15		In the forenoon Church Parade & Inspection of Billets by the C.O.	Appendix X
BRESLE	20/11/15		In the forenoon training as per programme. In the afternoon General Inspection by the Corps Commander	Appendices XI, XII & XIII + XIV
BRESLE	21/11/15		44th Inf. Bgde "Highland Games"	Appendix XV
BRESLE	22/11/15		Training as per programme	Appendix X
BRESLE	23/11/15		Training as per programme	

T/134. Wt. W708—776. 500000. 4/15. Sir J. C. & S.

Army Form C. 2118.

WAR DIARY
or
INTELLIGENCE SUMMARY.
(Erase heading not required.)

Instructions regarding War Diaries and Intelligence Summaries are contained in F. S. Regs., Part II. and the Staff Manual respectively. Title pages will be prepared in manuscript.

Place	Date	Hour	Summary of Events and Information	Remarks and references to Appendices
BRESLE	24/9/16		Training as per Programme. ŸB	Appendix X
BRESLE	25/9/16		Inspection of Billets by the S.O.C. Weather conditions interfered with training during the forenoon. Wiring drill in the afternoon. ŸB	Appendix XVI
BRESLE	26/9/16		Church Parades in the morning. Fire broke out in farm at N.W. side of village, in close proximity to Btn Sgts Mess. Ntn fire piquet on duty from about 1.30 P.M & throughout the night ŸB	Appendix XVII
BRESLE	27/9/16		The Btn was inspected by the Divisional Commander during the forenoon. ŸB	Appendix XVIII XIX & XX

T2134. Wt. W708—776. 500000. 4/15. Sir J. C. & S.

WAR DIARY
or
INTELLIGENCE SUMMARY.
(Erase heading not required.)

Army Form C. 2118.

Place	Date	Hour	Summary of Events and Information	Remarks and references to Appendices
BRESLE	28/11/16		Misty weather rendered impossible training in aeroplane contact work. Btn. paraded under B.S.M. for Sen drill & powders tested in the afternoon under the Bgde trading officer. YyB	
BRESLE	29/11/16		Btn. duty btn. & wholly employed on road fatigues in BRESLE & H.Q. Bgde. Bomb & Supply Dumps held in the afternoon. YyB	Appendix 31.
BRESLE	30/11/16		Commanding Officers parade in the forenoon. In the afternoon general cleaning up of billets etc preparatory to the Btn. moving to ALBERT on 1st Decr. YyB	

Appendix T

31/10/16

46th Inf. Bgde. ask for party of 250 o.r. & relative no. of officers for work on roads in CONTALMAISON. in vicinity of the CUTTING. Tools from R.E. Report to R.E. @ 8.30 A.M. to-morrow

SECRET   COPY NO ...7...

46th INFANTRY BRIGADE ORDER NO. 119.

Appendix II

Reference ALBERT
(combined sheet) 1/40,000   *Special*   1-11-16.

1. The 48th Division is relieving the 15th Division in front line. Two battalions of the 144th Infantry Brigade and two battalions of the 145th Infantry Brigade will relieve the 46th Infantry Brigade in the Reserve Brigade area to-day.

2. The 46th Infantry Brigade (less 10th Sco.Rif.) and 8th Seaforths attached will march to billets and bivouacs at BECOURT, ALBERT and MILLENCOURT in accordance with attached march table.

3. Lorries for Blankets will be at Camps of units at 8 p.m. as follows :--

LOZENGE WOOD	-	2 lorries
SCOTS REDOUBT	-	1 lorry
CONTALMAISON	-	1 lorry

Units to be on the look out for these lorries.

4. If units march off before Transport arrived, blankets will be collected in one place by units and loading parties left to load them.

5. Billeting parties will meet the Staff Captain as shewn in March Table.

6. Distances of 100 yards will be maintained between Platoons and equivalent units, 200 yards between Battalions on the march.
Platoons and equivalent unit Commanders will halt for 10 minutes at 10 minutes before each clock hour.

7. Guards will be left by units at Camps and Transport lines to take charge of all tents and camp equipment until taken over by relieving units. Guards will not march off until receipts have been obtained from an officer.

8. Only such transport as is required will accompany units on the march, remainder will march under the Brigade Transport Officer.

9. The extra day's rations in hand will be carried by units.

2.

10. Gumboots will be carried on Blanket lorries. Rations to-day will be delivered by supply wagons of the Train this evening in new areas. Rations will not be issued to-morrow.
Arrangements are being made to deliver blankets to 10th Sco.Rif. at BECOURT to-night.

11. On arrival at BECOURT tonight 10/Sco.R. & 8th Seaforths revert to command of their respective Brigadiers.

Captain,
Brigade Major,
46th Inf.Bde.

Issued at.... 12 Noon
through Signals.

```
Copy No  1   War Diary
         2   File
         3   7/8th K.O.Sco.Bord.
         4   10th Sco.Rif.
         5   10/11th High.L.I.
         6   12th High.L.I.
         7   8th Seaforth Hghrs.
         8   46th M.G. Coy.
         9   46th T.M.Battery
         10  Staff Captain
         11  Bde Transport Officer
         12  Bde Signal Officer
         13  Bde Supply Officer
         14  No 4 Coy.Train
         15  15th Division
         16  44th Inf.Bde
         17  45th Inf.Bde
         18  A.P.M., 15th Division.
```

HAIG H TABLE.

Issued with 46th Infantry Brigade Order No 119
dated 1-11-16.

Attached Appendix II

UNITS in order of march	STARTING POINT		ROUTE	DESTINATION	REMARKS
	Place	Time			
12th High.L.I.	Road junction X.27.b.2.0. LOZENGE WOOD	1.30 p.m.	Road (not shown on map) from LOZENGE WOOD to BECOURT - ARBRE TREULE - ALBERT CHURCH - Road junction W.23.c.1.1. X Road junction W.27.d.9.5. Follow road through E.1.7 and 8 to MILLENCOURT	MILLENCOURT	Billeting party to meet Staff Captain at Town Major's Office, MILLENCOURT at 3.30 p.m.
10/11th High.L.I.	"	2.10 p.m.	As above	"	"
46th M.G. Coy.	"	2.40 p.m.	As above	"	"
46th T.M.Battery	"	3.0 p.m.	As above	"	"
Brigade Head Quarters	"	3.5 p.m.	As above	"	"
7/8th K.O.Sco.Bord.	"	3.35 p.m.	As above as far as ALBERT	ALBERT	Billeting party to meet Staff Captain at Town Major's Office ALBERT at 2 p.m.
8th Seaforths	"	4.15 p.m.	As above as far as BECOURT	BECOURT	Billeting party to meet Staff Captain at BECOURT Cross Roads at 1 p.m. (X.25.d.5.6.)
1st Line Transport (not with units) under Bde Transport Officer.	BECOURT Cross Roads X.25.d.5.6.	1.30 p.m.		To destination as above.	This cancels previous instructions issued to Bde Transport Officer.

Ref'ce ALBERT Sheet   Map 1/40 000

The Battalion will march today as
under:—

Starting Point Batt'n H'quarters (X 16 D)
Time   9-40 a.m.
Route :–   PEAKE WOOD (X 22 A)
                LOZENGE WOOD (X 27 B)

Destination.   BECOURT.

Order of March:—   Batt H.Q.
                    A - Coy
                    B
                    C
                    D

Intervals.   100 yds between Platoons
                and similar units
                200 yds between Battalions

Baggage   will be collected & finished by 10
& Officers Kit and kept under a guard
                — They will be loaded
                at a lorrie which will call
                at Bn H.Q. at about 2 p.m.

Tents & Trench Stores
etc.   will be left in charge of a party
                from the Reserve
                & Relieving units 8th
                (Sussex Yorkshire Regt)
                Receipts will be taken
                for it today & forwarded
                as ordered to Brigade

Appendix III

"C" Form (Duplicate).
MESSAGES AND SIGNALS.

Army Form C. 2123.
(In books of 50's in duplicate.)

No. of Message ....

Charges to Pay. £ s. d.

Office Stamp. 1/11/16

Service Instructions. AR

Handed in at .... Office 4.40 p.m. Received 5.20 p.m.

TO DM

Sender's Number: BM560

AAA

Please detail daily party of 100 or to work on FRICOURT—CONTALMAISON road commencing tomorrow 2nd inst until further orders aaa Party to report to OC C Coy 2nd Latour Battalion at X27.B.1.1 at 6 am daily aaa Haversack rations to be taken as full days work will be done aaa Acknowledge aaa

FROM AR

PLACE & TIME

4 o/o perks

X 26 - 58
7.20
X roads   8 AM
Becourt Chateau
X 25 d 66

no tools Q.B.

Appendix IV

O.C. 8th Seaforths.

11th Brigade.

WORKING PARTY.

No. of Officers. 2
No. of Men. 100.
Date. 4th November 1916.
Time. 8.aaw.30am
Rendez-vous Own Traps office

To report to Tom Traps
Nature of work Earling damp at site
   & reinstating
Tools. Picks. 75 [?] 30 [?] Shovels.
Haversack Rations.

W. Waugh.
Captain,
Brigade Major,
11th Infantry Brigade.

3rd Nov. 1916.

appendix V

S E C R E T.   Copy No. 2

44th Infantry Brigade Operation Order No. 119.

4-11-16.

Reference Map:-
ALBERT Combined Sheet, 1/40,000.

1. The 44th Infantry Brigade will march to-morrow, 5th instant, to BRESLE, in accordance with March Table on reverse.

2. The following distances will be maintained throughout the whole march :-

    Between Battalions   -   200 yards.
    Between Platoons   -   100 yards.
    Between Sections M.G.Coy. -   100 yards.

3. Cookers and water-carts will follow in rear of their battalions.
    Remainder of transport to be brigaded and march 200 yards in rear of the T.M.Battery. There will be an interval of 100 yards between each regimental transport.

4. Billetting parties will meet the Staff Captain at the Town Major's Office, BRESLE, at 9 A.M.

5. Reports to head of column. Brigade Headquarters will open on arrival at the MAIRIE, BRESLE.

Issued at 6-30 P.M.
through Signals.

                                                            Lieut.
                                                    for Brigade Major,
                                                 44th Infantry Brigade.

Copies to :-

    No. 1. 9th Black Watch.
        2. 8th Seaforths.
        3. 8/10 Gordon Hrs.
        4. 7th Cameron Hrs.
        5. 44 M.G.Coy.
        6. 44 T.M.Battery.
        7. 15th Division.
        8. Bde. Transport Officer.
        9. "   Signalling Officer.
       10. Town Major, BECOURT.
       11. Town Major, BRESLE.
       12. Staff Captain.
       13. War Diary.
       14. File.

Appendix ?

MARCH TABLE TO ACCOMPANY 44TH INFANTRY BRIGADE O.O. No.119.

UNITS. In order of March.	Starting Point.	Time.	Route.
Brigade H.Qrs. and Sig.Secn:	X Roads at F.1.b.7.9. (At the foot of BECOURT Hill.)	A.M. 10-0	Road F.7.b.4.4. - E.12.a. - E.4.c. - E.4.b.3.3. - E.3.d.8.7. - Main ALBERT - AMIENS Road to Cross Roads at D.21.a.
7th Cameron Hrs.		10-2	
8/10th Gordons.		10-25	
8th Seaforth Hrs.		10-48	
9th Black Watch.		11-21	
44 M.G.Coy.		11-44	
44 T.M.Battery.		P.M. 12-1	
Brigaded Transport.		12-5	

Attach appendix V

44th Brigade B.M.28.

All Units 44th Inf.Bde.
Bde. Transport Officer.

Reference 44th Brigade Operation Order No. 119.
_____

1. Parties will halt independently at 10 minutes to the clock hour, and move off at the hour.

2. Units are reminded that huts must be left clean and areas tidy. Rear parties should be left for all clearing up.

3. Units will synchronize watches at Brigade Signal Office between 7-30 A.M. and 9 A.M.

4-11-18.

W Mackay Captain,
Brigade Major,
44th Infantry Brigade.

Appendix VI.

SECRET. Operation Order No. 43. Copy No. 9.

By Lieut Col R.C. Thomson D.S.O.
Commdg 8th Bn Seaforth Highlrs. 4-11-16

The Battn will march to BRESLE tomorrow 5-11-16 as follows:-

Starting Point:- BECOURT - LOZENGE WOOD ROAD at a point due South of the Camp
Time - 10-35 a.m.
Order of March:- Hqrs, C, A, D, B, Coy. L.G. Detatchment
Route - BECOURT - ALBERT - AMIENS ROAD

2. 100 yds interval will be maintained between platoons.

3. Cookers & water Carts will follow in rear of Battn. Remainder of Transport will be Brigaded.

4. Normal halts of 10 mins to each hour will be observed.

Brigade time will be obtained at Bde Signal Office between 7-30 a.m. & 9 a.m.

5. Advanced parties of 1 N.C.O. per Coy. + 1 for Hqrs will report to 2/Lt J.H. Ross at 8 a.m. at Q.M. Stores, RUE DEBUSSY, ALBERT, whence they will proceed on bicycles to BRESLE to meet the Staff Captn at the Town Majors office at 9 a.m.

H.H. Blackwood 2/Lieut
a/Adjt. 8th Seaforth Highldrs

Copy No 1 O.C. A Coy   6 Quartermaster
       2   B Coy   7 Indian Cavalry
       3   C Coy   8 2/Lt J.H. Ross
       4   D Coy   9 War Diary
       5 Transport Officer   10 File

War Diary

Appendix VII

8th (S) Battalion Seaforth Highlanders

Training Programme for Week Ending Nov. 12th 1916.

November	Morning	Afternoon	Night	Remarks
Monday – 6th	Cleaning up kit – Washing	Inspection and Improvement of Billets		
Tuesday – 7th	Individual & Section Training in Handling of Arms – Drill – Musketry – Bayonet Fighting – Physical Exercises.	Lectures by Company Commanders on Camp & Barrack duties, and on preservative measures against gas.	NIL.	
Wednesday – 8th	Do.	Lecture to Companies on Bombing – Lewis Guns and German Machine Guns.	NIL.	
Thursday – 9th	Do.	NIL.	Short night march by Sections on Compass Bearing or by given map References.	
Friday – 10th	Do.	Lectures by Coy. officers on field Engineering (Special attention to wiring revetments and construction of Strong Pts.)	NIL.	
Saturday – 11	Route march by Coys. on given map references.	Conference with Company Commanders on past and ensuing weeks work.	NIL.	
Sunday – 12th	Church Parade. Inspection of Billets by Commanding Officer.	NIL.	NIL.	

— November 6th 1916 —

J. Blackwood 2/Lt. and 2/adjutant
for Lieut. Col.
— Commdg. 8th Seaforth Highlanders —

War Diary

"C" Form (Duplicate).
MESSAGES AND SIGNALS.

Army Form C. 2123.
(In books of 50's in duplicate.)
No. of Message..........

		Charges to Pay.	Office Stamp.
SM MAM 43	2DD Kilpatrick	£ s. d.	D.M 9/11/16

Service Instructions. 7.DD

Handed in at......2DD......Office......m. Received 12.5 A.m.

Appendix VIII

TO ALL UNITS

Sender's Number	Day of Month	In reply to Number	A A A
SC 882	9/11	—	

The commander in chief will visit BRESLE at 2.45 this afternoon and troops will carry on with training programme and any men not employed will parade outside their billets as close as possible.

G Blackwood Lt
12.10 P.M 9/11/16

FROM .... B
PLACE & TIME .... 11.55 AM

8th BATTALION SEAFORTH HIGHLANDERS

TRAINING PROGRAMME — Week Ending Nov. 18th 1916

Appendix IX

Date	Morning	Afternoon	Night	Remarks
SUNDAY Nov. 12th	Church Parade. Inspection of Billets by C.O.	—	—	
MONDAY Nov. 13th	Route March by Coys. on given Map References.	Lecture by Coys. to Officers and N.C.O's on Map Reading.	—	
TUESDAY Nov. 14th	Platoon Training – Drill – Musketry – Bayonet Fighting – Physical Exercises – Special Jobs Training in Lewis Gun, Signalling, Bombing, Wiring, Patrolling – Use of Compass.	Lecture by Coy. Officers to N.C.O's only on Taping out a Strong Point by day or night.	—	
WEDNESDAY Nov. 15th	Do.	—	Short night march by Platoons on Compass Bearing or by given map References.	
THURSDAY Nov. 16th	Do. N.C.O's Taping out of Strong Points by Day.	Lecture by Coy.s. on "Sanitation" and "Prevention of Trench Feet".	—	
FRIDAY Nov. 17th	Do.	Lecture by Coy. Commanders on Camp and Barrack Duties and Preventative measures against Gas.	Officers and N.C.O's Taping out Strong Points by night.	
SATURDAY Nov. 18th	Do.	Conference with Coy. Commanders on past and ensuing Week's work.	—	

Nov. 11th 1916.

E. Alockwood
Lieut. & Adjutant
8th Seaforth Highrs. ¾ hour

Appendix X

8th Batn Seaforth Highrs
Training Programme — Week Ending — November 26th 1916.

Date	Morning	Afternoon	Night	Remarks
Sunday Nov 19th	Church Parade. Inspection of Billets	—	—	
Monday Nov 20th	(Company Training) Entrenching Drill. Tactical Handling of Platoons	Company Conference – Officers & N.C.O.'s discuss the Attack, to be carried out on 22nd inst.	—	
Tuesday Nov 21st	Brigade "Games"		—	
Wednesday Nov 22nd	The attack, up to and including the Assault, in the open. Cooperation of Lewis Guns - Stokes Guns and Scouts.	Company Conference – Officers & N.C.O.'s to discuss points in the attack, not brought forward on the ground. "Practice" T.S.R. 1 Chap 5.	—	
Thursday Nov 23rd	The Attack (Capture & Consolidation of Position). Sandbag Revetment.	Tactical exercise by Coy for Officers.	—	
Friday Nov 24th	Fire Control. Definition of Targets. Observing Covering Fire.	Discussion of Final Stage of Attack – Advanced Guards (Officers & N.C.O.'s)	—	
Saturday Nov 25th	Battalion Route March, Covered by Advance and Flank Guards.		—	

17th November 1916.

W. Mackintosh ?Col.
?Capt 8th Seaforth Highrs

Appendix XI

"C" Form (Original).
MESSAGES AND SIGNALS.

Army Form C. 2123.
(In books of 50's in duplicate.)

Prefix SM Code IGAM Words 26
Received From ZDD By Kilpatrick
Office Stamp SHH 20/11/16

Service Instructions. ZDD

Handed in at ZDD Office 9.35 A.m. Received 9.45 A.m.

TO: 8th Seaforths Hrs

Sender's Number: S/C 18
Day of Month: 20

AAA

1) Warning order army commander will inspect 44th brigade today aaa Time place and dress will be notified later

FROM PLACE & TIME: 44th I.B.

"C" Form (Original).
MESSAGES AND SIGNALS.

Army Form C. 2123.
(In books of 50's in duplicate.)

No. of Message: Appendix XII

Prefix SM	Code LCAM	Words 50	Received From ZDD	Sent or sent out	Office Stamp
Charges to collect			By KILPATRICK	At ... m. To ... By	SHH 20/11/16
Service Instructions ZDD					

Handed in at ZDD   Office 11·15 A.m.   Received 11·25 A.

TO ALL UNITS

Sender's Number	Day of Month	In reply to Number	AAA
SC24	20	—	

Ref. parade for army commander units will be drawn up on parade ground pointed out to adjutants this morning by brigade major at 3·15 P.M aaa Markers will report to brigade major at 3.PM aaa No officers will be mounted

FROM 44th I.B.

Appendix XIII

"C" Form (Original).
MESSAGES AND SIGNALS.

Army Form C. 2123.
(In books of 50's in duplicate.)

No. of Message ....

| Prefix SM | Code LKAM | Words 25 | Received From ZDD By KILPATRICK | Sent, or sent out At .... m. To .... By .... | Office Stamp. SHH 20/11/16 |

Charges to collect ....

Service Instructions. ZDD

Handed in at ZDD .... Office 11·50 A.m. Received 11·56 A.m.

TO: 8TH SEAFORTH HRS

| *Sender's Number SC 31 | Day of Month 20 | In reply to Number | AAA |

Dress for parade this afternoon will be side arms and waist belt aaa Rifles will not be carried aaa

Later instructions are that rifles are to be carried

FROM PLACE & TIME: 44th I.B.

8th. BATTALION SEAFORTH HIGHLANDERS.

Appendix XIV

O.C. all Coys.
L.G.O.
Transport Officer.
Battalion Sgt. Major.

1. The Corps Commander will inspect the Brigade this afternoon.

2. The Battalion will parade for sizing purposes at 2.45. p.m. in the field where Church Parades are held.

3. DRESS. OFFICERS. Belts and sticks. No Officers to be mounted.
   OTHER RANKS. Belts and Side-Arms. ~~No Rifles.~~

4. Every available man is to parade; specialists to parade with their Coys.
   2 Cooks, 2 Officers servants, per Coy., and 1 man per Billet may be left behind.
   All working parties, with the exception of the 6 men working under the direction of Major McLeod of the Cameron Hrs., are cancelled.
   Parade States showing the number of men on and off Parade to be produced.

5. The Battalion Sgt. Major will detail 2 markers to meet the Brigade Major at 3 p.m. on the ground to the south of the lower football pitch.

6. When the Coys. have been equalised and sized, the Battalion will be marched to the parade ground where it will be formed up in close column of Coys.

.......H.Blackwood........ 2/Lieut.,
a/Adjutant 8th. Seaforth Highrs.

Appendix XV

PROGRAMME.

44TH "HIGHLAND" BRIGADE GAMES.   To be held on 21st Novbr., 1916.

TIME.	EVENTS.	PRIZES.

FOOTBALL. 11 a side. Company teams.   110 Fcs. to
   One company team from each unit.   winning team.
   Finals will be played on the 20th Nov.

A.M.   Fcs.

10-0 (1) TUG-OF-WAR. First round.   1st. 10. (Each man
     (Teams of 10 men and coach).   2nd. 5. (& coach.

10-15 (2) HIGH JUMP. Entries - 4 from each   1st. 25.
     battn., and 1 from each other   2nd. 15.
  unit.   3rd. 5.
     6 best to be left in for Final.

10-30 (3) 100 YARDS. Entries - 4 from each   1st. 25.
     battn., and 1 from each other unit. 2nd. 15.
   6 best to be left in for Final.   3rd. 5.

11-0 (4) LONG JUMP. Entries - 4 from each   1st. 25.
     battn., and 1 from each other unit. 2nd. 15.
   6 best to be left in for Final.   3rd. 5.

11-0 (5) PIPING & DANCING. (Continuous).
     Piping.
       March.   1st. 25.
       Strathspey.   2nd. 15.
       Reel.

     Dancing.
       Foursome.- One set from each   1st. 40.
         battn. or other unit.   2nd. 20.
       Highland Fling.- 2 from each   1st. 20.
         battn. or other unit.   2nd. 20.
       Sword Dance.- 2 from each   1st. 20.
         battn. or other unit.   2nd. 15.
        (Pipe Majors are excluded).

11-30 (6) TUG-OF-WAR. Semi-Finals.

NOON.
12-0 (7) PUTTING THE WEIGHT.
      4 entries from each battn., and   1st. 25.
  1 from other units.   2nd. 15.
  6 best to be left in for Finals.   3rd. 5.

-------- I N T E R V A L. --------

P.M.
2-0 (8) HIGH JUMP. Finals.

    (9) 100 YARDS. Finals.

   (10) PIPING & DANCING. (Continuous).

2-30 (11) TOSSING THE CABER.   1st. 25.
      2 entries from each battn.,   2nd. 15.
  and 1 from other units.   3rd. 5.

2-30 (12) MILE RACE.   1st. 30
      4 entries from each battn., and 2nd. 20.
  1 from other units.   3rd. 10.

2-45 (13) PUTTING THE WEIGHT. Finals.

                                                                          P.T.O.

P.M.

2-45 (14) "V.C". RACE. Officers mounted.
 Entries unlimited (subject to
 condition of ground).

                                        Fcs.

3-0 (15) RELAY RACE.
 One team from each unit. Teams to   1st. 100.)
 consist of Company Commander, Subaltern,   2nd. 60.) To O.R.
 C.S.M., or C.Q.M.S., Sgt., Cpl., or L.Cpl. 3rd. 20.)
 and Private. (Battalion teams to belong
 to one Company).

3-15 (16) OBSTACLE RACE.   1st. 20.
 Entries unlimited.   2nd. 10.

3-30 (17) CROSS COUNTRY RACE. About 2½ miles.   1st. 30.
 Entries (unlimited) open to battns.   2nd. 25.
 First 20 will count in allotting Points   3rd. 20.
 to Battalions - independently of mens   4th. 15.
 prizes.   5th. 10.

3-30 (18) BEST TURNED-OUT LIMBERED WAGON. With   1st. 30.
 drivers and brakesmen in marching
 order.
 BEST M.G.CREW. in fighting order - to   1st. 30.
 bring gun in and out of action.
 BEST G.S.WAGON. - with drivers and   1st. 30.
 brakesmen in marching order.

3-45 (19) LONG JUMP. Finals.

3-45 (20) TUG-OF-WAR. Finals.

4-0 (21) OFFICERS OBSTACLE RACE.

The Silver Bugle given by Brigadier General M.G.WILKINSON, C.B., M.V.O. - the late Commander of the Brigade - will be competed for by the battalions.
The following points will be given :-

1st Prize.	2nd Prize.	3rd Prize.
5 points.	3 points.	1 point.

and the following will be Championship Events :-

    100 Yards.   Cross Country Race.
    Mile Race.   Football.
    Tossing the Caber.   Long Jump.
    Tug-of-War.   High Jump.
    Putting the Weight.

Copy forward at 9 am ~~Orders~~ W
~~C.O.~~

Appendix VI

"C" Form (Duplicate).
MESSAGES AND SIGNALS.

Army Form C.2123
(In books of 50's in duplicate.)

No. of Message ....

SM KAMY40 401B Lyn

Charges to Pay. £ s. d.

Office Stamp.
SH IT
23/11/16

Service Instructions. ZDB

Handed in at 441 B Signal Office 9.50 a.m. Received 10.15 a.m.

TO 5th SEAFORTHS

Sender's Number	Day of Month	In reply to Number	A A A
SC 49	23		

The brigade commander will go round billets on saturday 25th inst beginning at machine gun coy at 9.30 AM AAA Officers commanding units will meet the brigade commander in their own area AAA

FROM
PLACE & TIME
441 B
9.50 AM

Appendix XVII

8th Battalion "Seaforth" Highlanders.

Training - Programme - for Week Ending Nov Dec 2nd 1916

DATE	MORNING	AFTERNOON	NIGHT	REMARKS
SUNDAY - Nov 26th	9am to 11am 11.15am to 12.30am CHURCH PARADE			
MONDAY - Nov 27th	Battalion as Advance Guard to Brigade.	2.15 p.m. Officers discussion of Tactical Exercise, Selection of Defensive Position, between BRESLE WOOD and LAVIEVILLE.		
TUESDAY - Nov 28th	Battalion Coy. Officers tactical exercise. Selection of Position and "taking up of Battalion as Outpost on line FRANVILLERS - BRESLE WOOD			
WEDNESDAY - Nov 29th	Battalion at Night Outposts to Brigade			
THURSDAY - Nov 30th	Battalion acting as Rearguard to Retirement of Brigade	Officers - Reconnaissance and road report between BRESLE, BAIZIEUX, WARLOY, HARPONVILLE.		
FRIDAY - Dec 1st	Battalion in the Assault. Reforming.			
SATURDAY - Dec 2nd	Inspection of Billets			

Under Coy. Arrangements for Bayonet fighting; Musketry; Physical Training; Preventative measures against Gas; Revetments; Wiring.

Nov. 25th 1916

G. Blackwood 2/Lieut,
Adjutant, 8th Seaforth Highlanders.

URGENT.

Appendix XVIII

44th Brigade B.M. 29/2.

All Units 44th I. B.
----

1. The G.O.C. will carry out the following inspections on Monday November 27th.

2. (i) When inspecting, the G.O.C. wishes to see in each Battalion :-
    (a) Whole Battalion on parade as strong as possible :-

        One Company in Drill Order.
        Two companies in marching order.
        One Company in fighting order with full size tools.
        Lewis Guns to be with their companies,
        Battalion section in marching order.
    (b) One company - platoon and company drill.
    (c) One company on the range (individual and collective) and bombing squads bombing.
    (d) One company marking out a strong point, cruciform pattern, or wiring.
    (e) One company physical training, bayonet fighting and preparation of feet for trenches.

(ii) Machine Gun Company and Trench Mortar Battery in marching order (complete).

3. The following is a draft Time-table of G.O.C's inspection :-
        8-30 a.m. 9th Black Watch.
        9-0 a.m. 7th Cameron Highrs.
        10-30 a.m. 8th Seaforth Highrs.
        12 Noon   44th Trench Mortar Battery.
        12-20 p.m. 44th Machine Gun Company.
        2-0 p.m. 9/10th Gordon Highrs.

Battalions will be inspected on their own parade ground.

4. Details will be issued on 26th November.

Captain,
Brigade Major,
44th Infantry Brigade.

26th Novr. 1916.

5th. BATTALION SEAFORTH HIGHLANDERS

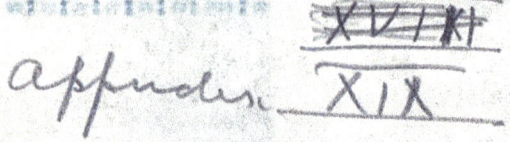

O.C. all Companies.
Lewis Gun Officer.
2/Lieut. R.V.Cuthbert.
War Diary.
File.

Reference previous communication, the Battalion will be inspected to-morrow as follows:-

"A" Company.   in DRILL ORDER.
"B" Company.   FIGHTING ORDER with full sized tools.
"C" Company.   MARCHING ORDER.
"D" Company.   MARCHING ORDER.

All specialists will parade with their Companies, with the exception of the Pipers and Drummers, and the Headquarters Lewis Gun Section. The Headquarters Lewis Gun Section will parade in marching order.

Left Markers, one from each Company, will be on the Parade Ground at 9.45 a.m. The Battalion will form up in mass at 9.45 a.m.

Lewis Gun Sections of each Company will parade 10 paces in rear of their Companies.
Headquarters Lewis Gun Section will parade 15 paces in the rear of the Battalion.

At 10.30 a.m.- the Battalion will be inspected in Mass.

At 11./0.a.m.- "D" Company will be inspected in Drill.

At 11.15 a.m.- "A" Company will be inspected in- (a) Physical Training.
                                                  (b) Bayonet Exercise.
                                                  (c) Preparation of feet for trenches.

At 11.30 a.m.- "B" Company. One half of Company will be inspected in Wiring and the other half in marking out Strong Points.

At 11.45 a.m.- "C" Company. will be inspected on the Range-(individual and collective) and Bombing Squads Bombing.

2/Lieut. R.V.Cuthbert will continue with his Tunnelling instruction. He will have two men as instructors and will notify O.sC.Companies of the names of those men.

------------------ oOo ------------------

                                        George W. Duncan
                                        ....Captain,
Nov. 15th. 1915.   Adjutant 5th. Battn. Seaforth Highlanders.

Appendix XX

Inspection of 44th Infantry Brigade
by
G.O.C., 15th Division. Monday 27th Nov. 1916.
Vide: B.M. 29/8 d/25.11.16.

TIME.	UNIT.	EXERCISE.	COMPANY.	DRESS.	Remarks.
8-30 a.m.	9th Black Watch.	Inspection.	-	F.O.	
8-40 a.m.	- do -	Drill	-	F.O.	
9-0 a.m.	7th Cameron Hrs.	Inspection.	A. / B.C. / D.	F.O. / M.O. / D.O.	
9-30 a.m.	- do -	Drill.	B.		
9-45 a.m.	- do -	½ Wiring / ½ Marking out.	A.		
10-0 a.m.	- do -	Physical Training / Bayonet Exercise / Feet Prevention.	D.		
10-10 a.m.	x xx x	Bombing.	Bomb.Squads. 9th B.Watch. "C" Coy. 7th Camerons.		
10-20 a.m.	7th Cameron Hrs.	Range.	C.		
10-30 a.m.	8th Seaforth Hrs.	Inspection.	A. / B. / C.D.	D.O. / F.O. / M.O.	
11-0 a.m.	- do -	Drill	D.		
11-15 a.m.	- do -	Physical Trng. / Bayonet Exer. / Feet Prevent.	A.		
11-30 a.m.	- do -	½ Wiring. / ½ Marking out.	B.		
11-45 a.m.	- do -	Range.	C.		
12 NOON	44th T. M. Battery.	Inspection.	-		
12-10 p.m.	- do -	Firing.			
12-20 p.m.	44th M. G. Company.	Inspection.			
12-30 p.m.	- do -	Firing.			
2-0 p.m.	8/10th Gordon Hrs.	Inspection.	A.D. / C. / B.	M.O. / F.O. / D.O.	
2-30 p.m.	- do -	Drill.	A.		
2-45 p.m.	- do -	½ Wiring. / ½ Marking out.	C.		
3-0 p.m.	- do -	Physical Trng. / Bayonet Ex. / Feet Prevent.	B.		
3-20 p.m.	- do -	Range.	D.		
3-30 p.m.	- do -	Bombing.	D.		

F.O. = Fighting Order.
M.O. = Marching Order.
D.O. = Drill Order.

26th Nov. 1916.

Captain,
Brigade Major,
44th Infantry Brigade.

Copies to :

All Units 44th I. B.
H.Q. 15th Division - for information.

8th Battalion Seaforth Highlanders.

Casualties during the month of
NOVEMBER, 1916.

-:-

Officers. Killed.................. Nil.
Officers.. Wounded................ Nil.

Other Ranks. 1st November...........1. Wounded.
            4th November...........1.   "
                                            2

In the Field.
30/11/1916.

                                      ....2/Lieut.
          8th Battalion Seaforth Highlanders.

CONFIDENTIAL.

WAR DIARY.

8th (Ser) Battalion. Seaforth Highlanders.

From 1st Decr 1916 to 31st Decr. 1916 inclusive

(Volumn 18)

In the Field.
31/12/1916.

N.P. Swinburne Major for .... Lt Colonel.
Comdg; 8th (Ser) Battalion Seaforth Highlanders.

Headquarters.
15th Division.

Herewith War Diary for the month of December, 1916.   Kindly acknowledge receipt.

In the Field.
31/12/1916.

W. R. Swinburne
...x. Major. for. Lt Colonel.
Comdg; 8th Bn. Seaforth Highlanders.

WAR DIARY
or
INTELLIGENCE SUMMARY.
(Erase heading not required.)

Army Form

Instructions regarding War Diaries and Intelligence Summaries are contained in F. S. Regs., Part II. and the Staff Manual respectively. Title pages will be prepared in manuscript.

Place	Date	Hour	Summary of Events and Information	Remarks and references to Appendices
BRESLE	1/12/16		The Btn. moved to billets in ALBERT in accordance with 44th Inf. Bgde. operation order no. 120 & Btn. O.O. no 44. GM	Appendices I, II, III
ALBERT	2/12/16		Btn. billets inspected by G.O.C. Btn. "Duty Stn." The whole Btn. employed on guards & fatigues in accordance with 44th Bgde. BM 31/16. GM	Appendices IV, V, VI & VII
ALBERT	3/12/16		Church Parades in the forenoon in accordance with programme. Btn. had use of Divisional Baths from 8 A.M. – 5 P.M. ALBERT shelled for an hour from 4 P.M. about 20 shells fell. No damage within Btn. billeting area. GM	Appendix VIII & Appendix IX
ALBERT	4/12/16		Training as per programme. Orders issued on arrangements in event of town being shelled Orders for bays reconnaissance of localities in Corps area. GM	Appendix VII, X & XI

T2134. Wt. W708—776. 500000. 4/15. Sir J. C. & S.

WAR DIARY
or
INTELLIGENCE SUMMARY

Army Form C. 2118.

Place	Date	Hour	Summary of Events and Information	Remarks and references to Appendices
ALBERT	5/12/16		Working party of 4 officers + 200 o.r. reported to Town Major. Remainder of Btn. training as per programme. Warning order recd. of move to MAMETZ WOOD. O.O. recd. later for move on 7 inst.	Appendix XII Appendix XIII 94/B
ALBERT	6/12/16		Btn. duty Btn. + wholly employed on fatigues	Appendix XIV XV 94/B
ALBERT	7/12/16		Btn. moved to camp at X.23 central near South West corner of MAMETZ WOOD and took over from the 13th Btn. the Royal Scots in accordance with 44 Inf. Bgde. Operation order no. 12) and Btn. operation order no. 45.) Relief reported complete at 7.46 P.M. Camp very inaccessible + poorly equipped.	Appendix XVI + XVII 94/B
X.2.3 CENTRAL	8/12/16		Btn. employed on working parties 1 officer + 50 o.r. refered to 2nd Lt. Storm + party Dvpt. R.E. on extn. of MAMETZ WOOD at a point X.18 c.8.3. Remainder	

WAR DIARY
or
INTELLIGENCE SUMMARY.

Army Form C. 2118.

Place	Date	Hour	Summary of Events and Information	Remarks and references to Appendices
X.2,3 CENTRAL	8/12/16 (cont)		remainder of Btn. with 3 officers reported to O.C. 3/1st S.M. Field Coy R.E. at R.E. Dump about X.18.b.9.5. for work on roads. Test carried out regarding speed of advance of infantry in fighting order over broken ground. Test by D Coy 9th. Three reliefs of one officer & 10 men working on dug outs near HIGH WOOD for instructional purposes only.	Appendix XVIII Appendix XIX
X.2,3 CENTRAL	9/12/16		Btn. employed on fatigues as on previous day. Instructional reliefs on HIGH WOOD dug outs as on 8th inst. 9th	
X.2,3 CENTRAL	10/12/16		Btn. employed on fatigues as on previous day. A certain number of men in each Btn. could very profitably be given instruction in charcoal burning as this training is of great use in camp & in the trenches. The instruction in dugout making &c. 9th	
X.2,3 CENTRAL	11/12/16		Btn. employed on fatigues as on previous day. 9th	

Army Form C. 2118.

WAR DIARY
or
INTELLIGENCE SUMMARY.
(Erase heading not required.)

Instructions regarding War Diaries and Intelligence Summaries are contained in F.S. Regs., Part II. and the Staff Manual respectively. Title pages will be prepared in manuscript.

Place	Date	Hour	Summary of Events and Information	Remarks and references to Appendices
X.2.3. CENTRAL	12/2/16		Work parties as previous day cancelled during forenoon on account of inclement weather. A further party of 2 officers & 100 o.r. reported to O/C Bottom Wood Dump but dismissed on account of weather & ordered to report at 8.30 A.M. on 13th inst.	
X.2.3. CENTRAL	13/2/16		Work parties 1 off & 50 men reported to officer of R.E. at X18C6.3 in Mametz Wood. 2 off & 100 o.r. reported to O/C Bottom Wood Dump. Remainder of Bn. under 2 officers reported to O/C 2/1 ½ S.M. Field Coy R.E. at about S13.b9.5	
X.2.3. CENTRAL	14/2/16		Work parties as yesterday but party reporting to O/C Bottom Wood Dump reduced to 1 off & 50 men	

T2134. Wt. W708—776. 500000. 4/15. Sir J. C. & S.

WAR DIARY
or
INTELLIGENCE SUMMARY.

Army Form C. 2118.

Place	Date	Hour	Summary of Events and Information	Remarks and references to Appendices
X.2.3. Central	15/12/15		Btn. employed on working parties as on previous day. GWB	
X.2.3 Central	16/12/15		Btn. employed on working parties as on previous day. 100 o.r. detained for removal of stores etc. to new camp. In accordance with 24th Inf Bde O.O. no 122 & Btn O.O. no 46 Btn. moved to huts at SHELTER WOOD SOUTH. Transport did not move. GWB	Appendix XX XXI Appendix XXII
SHELTER WOOD	17/12/15		Btn. Btn on duty. Working party of 160 reported at LANGLAND CIRCUS & one of 40 at CONTALMAISON. Btn transport moved to CHAPES SPUR. GWB	Appendix XVIII " XIX
SHELTER WOOD	18/12/15		Working parties in camp organizing drainage etc. GWB	

WAR DIARY
or
INTELLIGENCE SUMMARY.
(Erase heading not required.)

Army Form C. 2118.

Place	Date	Hour	Summary of Events and Information	Remarks and references to Appendices
SHELTER WOOD	19/2/16		Working parties in Camp in forenoon under Bn. arrangements. In accordance with 44th Inf. Bgde O.O no 123 and Bn. O.O. no 47 17th Bn relieved the 6/7th R.S.F in support. A & C Coys in 26th AVENUE and B & D Coys in MARTINPUICH. Trenches in a very bad state of repair. In carrying sheds in the Brigade area. Bn. H.Qrs in 26th AVENUE M21 d 3.0	Appendix XXIV + XXV & XXVI + XXVII
26th AVENUE	20/2/16		Improvement of trenches and dug-outs under Bn. arrangements. Working party of 3 officers + 100 men on work in GILBERT ALLEY for four hours 5 P.M - 9 P.M. Casualties Wounded O.R. 2	
26th AVENUE	21/2/16		In accordance with 44th Inf. Bgde. O.O. no. 124, Bn. O.O no 48 and 6/16th Gordon Hders O.O S.H. 39 Bn. relieved 6/16th Gordons in front line to the extent of a five-platoon front. D Coy in front line. C Coy with one platoon on left flank + having a flank front line other 3 platoons in reserve	Appendix XXVIII + XXIX + XXX

WAR DIARY or INTELLIGENCE SUMMARY

Army Form C. 2118.

Place	Date	Hour	Summary of Events and Information	Remarks and references to Appendices
26 AVENUE	21/2/16 (cont)		Working party of 1 officer & 60 o.r. on work in GILBERT ALLEY from 10 P.M. till 2 A.M. Another working party of 1 officer & 45 O.R. on work in SHELTER TRENCH at M15 c 6:3. supplied by C Coy. Bn HQ as remained in 26th AVENUE $44A$	
26 AVENUE	22/2/16		In accordance with Bn. O.O. no 47 "A" Coy. relieved "D" Coy in the firing line. One officer & 6 O.R's of "B" Coy on work in GILBERT ALLEY and SHELTER TRENCH under the R.E. Tour hours work put in Wounded O.R. 2 $44B$	Appendix XXXVI
26 AVENUE	23/2/16		In accordance with 44th Inf. Bde. O.O. no 125 & Bn. o.o. no 50 the Bn. was relieved by the 9th Bn. Black Watch. Btn. moved into ACID DROP SOUTH. Bn. in camp by 10 P.M. Wounded O.R. 6 $44B$	Appendices XXXVII & XXXVIII

Army Form C. 2118.

WAR DIARY
or
INTELLIGENCE SUMMARY.
(Erase heading not required.)

Instructions regarding War Diaries and Intelligence Summaries are contained in F.S. Regs., Part II. and the Staff Manual respectively. Title pages will be prepared in manuscript.

Place	Date	Hour	Summary of Events and Information	Remarks and references to Appendices
ACID DROP SOUTH	24/12/15		Kit, rifles, bombs & ammunition inspection under Coy arrangements. Wounded O.R. 2 JJB	
ACID DROP SOUTH	25/12/15		In accordance with 44th Inf Bgde O.O. no. 126 & Btn o.o. no. 51 the Btn relieved the 7th Bn. Cameron Hlders in the right sub-section of the Bgde front. Btn. HQrs moved to 36th AVENUE, 7th Bn Cameron Hldrs O.O. 7 herewith. Wounded O.R. 1 Missing O.R. 3 JJB	appendices XXIV XXXV XXXVI
36th AVENUE	26/12/15		In accordance with Btn. O.O. no. 52 "C" Coy relieved "B" Coy in the front line. Wounded O.R. 1 JJB	appendices XXXVII
36th AVENUE	27/12/15		In accordance with 44th Bgde. O.O. no 127 and Btn O.O. no 53 the Btn was relieved by the 13th Btn H.L.I. and on relief moved to SHELTER WOOD and took over from the 7/8th K.O.S.B. Wounded O.R. 1 JJB	appendices XXXVIII, XXXIX

T2134. Wt. W708—776. 500000. 4/15. Sir J.C. & S.

WAR DIARY
or
INTELLIGENCE SUMMARY.
(Erase heading not required.)

Army Form C. 2118.

Place	Date	Hour	Summary of Events and Information	Remarks and references to Appendices
SHELTER WOOD SOUTH	28/12/16		Rifle & gas helmet inspections under Coy arrangements. YYA	
SHELTER WOOD SOUTH	29/12/16		Btn. engaged on Comp. improvement & drainage under 2nd Lt. Cuthbert. YYA	
SHELTER WOOD SOUTH	30/12/16		Btn. Ats. on duty & fully employed on working parties. YYA	
SHELTER WOOD SOUTH	31/12/16		In accordance with 44th Inf. Bde. O.O. no. 128 & Btn. O.O. no. 54 the Btn. relieved the 13th Bn. the Royal Scots in support. Btn. H.Qrs at SEVEN ELMS M28d central. "A" Coy in PRUE TRENCH "B" Coy at SEVEN ELMS "C" & "D" Coys in STARFISH TRENCH. YYA	Appendices XL & XLI

Casualties during the month of December, 1916.

Officers Killed. NIL.
Officers Wounded. NIL.
Officers Missing. NIL

Other Ranks Killed. NIL.
Other Ranks Wounded =

    20th December. = 2.
    22nd   "   = 3.
    23rd   "   = 6.
    24th   "   = 2.
    25th   "   = 1.
    26th   "   = 1.
    27th   "   = 1.

    Total = **45.**

Other Ranks Missing =

    25th December. = 3.

In the Field.
31-12-1916.

                                                                                                                       W Blackwood   2/Lt A/Adj.
                8th Bn. Seaforth Highlanders.

Appendix I

S E C R E T.   COPY No. 2

44TH INFANTRY BRIGADE OPERATION ORDER No.120.

th November 1916.

Reference Map:
ALBERT Combined Sheet 1/40,000.

1. The 15th Division will relieve the 50th Division in the Corps Support Area on the 30th November and 1st December.

2. The 44th Infantry Brigade will relieve the 149th Infantry Brigade in billets in ALBERT on the 1st December and will march in accordance with the accompanying Table.

3. Transport will march in rear of Units.

4. During all movements, distances of 200 yards are to be maintained between Battalions, and 100 yards between platoons and units of equivalent road space.

5. Billeting parties will meet the Staff Captain at the Town Major's Office, ALBERT at 10-30 a.m. 30th instant. Parties will be billeted in ALBERT that night.

6. All ovens and general improvements under-construction should be handed over to relieving units.

7. Brigade Headquarters will close at BRESLE and open simultaneously at No. 88 RUE DE BAPAUME, ALBERT.

Issued through
Signals.

_____ P.M.

Captain,
Brigade Major,
44th Infantry Brigade.

Copy No. 1. 9th Black Watch.
2. 9th Seaforth Highrs.
3. 8/10th Gordon Highrs.
4. 7th Cameron Highrs.
5. 44th M. G. Company.
6. 44th T. M. Battery.
7. H.Q. 15th Division.
8. 45th Inf. Bde.
9. 46th Inf. Bde.
10. 149th Inf. Bde.
11. Bde. Transport Officer.
12. Bde. Supply Officer.
13. Bde. Signal Officer.
14. No. 2 Coy. Train.
15. Staff Captain.
16. War Diary.
17. File.

MARCH TABLE to accompany 11th Infantry Brigade Operation Order No. 120 dated 28.11.16.

UNIT.	STARTING POINT.	TIME.	ROUTE.	REMARKS.
Brigade H.Qrs. and Signal Secn:	T Roads at J.10.a.0.0.9.	8-0 a.m.	LAVIEVILLE - MILLENCOURT - ALBERT.	
8/10th Gordon Hrs.		8-2 a.m.		
8th Seaforth Hrs.		8-27 a.m.		
9th Black Watch.		8-52 a.m.		
7th Cameron Hrs.		9-0 a.m.		
11th M.G. Company.		9-25 a.m.		
11th T.M. Battery.		9-42 a.m.		

SECRET

COPY No. 10

Appendix II

OPERATION ORDER No. 44

by

Lieut. Col. N. A. Thomson, D.S.O.,

Commdg. 8th (S). Battalion Seaforth Highlanders

Ref. Map. - ALBERT (Combined) Sheet 1/40,000   Nov. 30th 1916.

1. The Battalion will march to-morrow, to ALBERT, as follows:-

   STARTING POINT - CROSS ROADS - 200 yds. East of the CHURCH, BRESLE.

   TIME .... 8.15 a.m.

   ORDER OF MARCH - "D", "A", "B", and "C" Coys.

   ROUTE - LAVIEVILLE, MILLENCOURT, ALBERT.

   All movements will be by platoons at 100 yards interval.

2. All Blankets will be rolled in bundles of ten, labelled and stacked in Quartermaster's Stores by 6.30 a.m.

   Officers Valises will be in Quartermasters Stores by 7.30 a.m.

   Mess Boxes will be collected at 7.45 a.m.

3. First Line Transport will march in rear of the Battalion.

   2/Lieut. R.V. Cuthbert will march in rear of the Transport, with all details.

   Not more than 2 cooks will march with each cooker and one brakesman with each waggon.

   The Transport Officer will arrange to send back any men who may fall out to report to this Officer.

                                            G. Blackwood   2/Lieut.
                                      for Adjutant, 8th Seaforth Highlanders.

DISTRIBUTION - COPY. No. (1). O.C. "A" Coy.   (6). Sigs. Officer
                         (2) O.C. "B" Coy.   (7) Quartermaster.
                         (3) O.C. "C" Coy.   (8) Transport Officer.
                         (4) O.C. "D" Coy.   (9) 2nd in Command.
                         (5) L.G.O.   (10) War Diary.
                              (11) FILE.

Issued through Signals at... 11.30 a.m.

Headquarters,
8th. Seaforth Hrs.

Appendix III

All Recipients of O.O. No. 44.

If it is dry to-morrow morning, blankets and Officers Vallees will be taken to the SQUARE and not to the Quartermasters Stores.

If wet, they will be taken to the Quartermasters Stores. O.s C. Companies are reminded that all Billets, Latrines, etc, must be left scrupulously clean. They will be inspected by an Officer before the Battalion vacates this area. Certificates to this effect will be rendered to Battalion Headquarters. O.s C. Coys. will also leave behind 1 N.C.O. per Coy. to report to Quartermaster at 7.45 a.m. to-morrow.

Nov. 30th. 1918.

..................Capt.,
Adjutant 8th. Bn. Seaforth Highlanders.

O.C. All Coys.
Quartermaster.

    The Brigade Commander will inspect the Billets at 11.A.M. to-morrow.
    All Billets must be thoroughly cleaned before the Working Parties leave to-morrow morning.
    One Officer per Company must be in the Company Lines at that hour.
    The Quartermaster will attend.

In the Field.
1/12/1916.

.... Captain.
Adjutant, 8th Battn. Seaforth Highlanders.

Appendix IV

U R G E N T. 44th Brigade. B.M.31/16.

Appendix V

O. C., ~~9th Black Watch~~,
     8th Seaforth Highrs.,
     ~~8/10th Gordon Highrs.~~,
     ~~7th Cameron Highrs~~.

1.   44th Brigade B.M. 31/15 dated 28th Novr. is cancelled.

2.   The following working parties and guard now being carried out by the 50th Division will be taken over by the Brigade commencing 7-30 a.m. on 2nd December.

  (i)   1 Officer and 110 O.R. to report to O.C. "G" Dump at E.9.D. Central for work at R.E. Stores.

  (ii)   1 Officer and 40 O.R. to take over guard on German prisoners at E.3.A.

  (iii)   4 Officers and 200 O.R. to report to O.C. "D" Company, 2nd Labour Battalion at 8 a.m. at Level Crossing of Metre Gauge Railway on ALBERT - BAPAUME Road for work on that road.

  (iv)   1 N.C.O. and 20 men to report at Coal Dump, ALBERT at 10-0 a.m. Tools required - 20 shovels.

The above will be carried out daily by the Duty Battalion for the day.

3.   The battalion next for duty will detail for the day previous to coming on duty -

    4 Officers and 200 men to report at Town Major's office at 8 a.m.

No tools required.

4.   Duty Battalion will be found as follows :-

    Decr. 2nd.   8th Seaforth Highrs.
    "   3rd   8/10th Gordon Highrs.
    "   4th   7th Cameron Highrs.
    "   5th   9th Black Watch.

and in rotation.

                               Captain,
                            Brigade Major,
1st December 1916.   44th Infantry Brigade.

Appendix VI

D.3.

O.C.All Coys.
Signalling Officer.
----

1. The following Working Parties will be found tomorrow as under :-

(a)   1 Officer & 100 O.R. "B"Coy.
               10.O.R. "D"Coy.
This party will parade at 6-30.A.M.under the Officer detailed by O.C."B"Coy & will report to O.C."G"Dump at E.9.d.Central at 7-30.A.M.for work at R.E.Store.
Tools - Nil. Dress - Skeleton Equipment.

(b)   1 Officer & 40.O.R. "D"Coy.

This party will parade at 6-30.A.M.& will report to E.3.a at 7-30.A.M.to take over Guard on German Prisoners
Dress - Skeleton equipment.

(c)   2 Officers & 80.O.R. "A"Coy.
      1 Officer   & 40.O.R. "D"Coy.
      1 Officer   & 80.O.R. "C"Coy.

This party will be under Captain G Murray & will parade at 6-45.A.M.& will report to O.C."D"Coy 2nd Labour Bn. at 7-30.A.M.for work on the ALBERT BAPAUME ROAD.
Dress - Skeleton Equipment.

(d) 1 N.C.O & 20 O.R to be found by Battalion Signallers.
This party will parade at Bn Hd Qrs at 9-30.A.M.
Dress - Clean Fatigue Dress.
20 Shovels to be drawn from the Qr Mr Stores.

2. All the above parties except(d)will carry Haversack Rations

3. Officers i/c Parties can see the Map to which above coordinates refer at Bn Hd Qrs.

In the Field.
1/12/1916.

                              .... Captain.
                   Adjutant.8th Bn.Seaforth Highlanders.

Appendix VII

D.3.

O.C.All Coys.
Signalling Officer.

Reference Working Parties for tomorrow as detailed in this Office D.3 -

Party of 4 Officers & 200 Other Ranks under Capt.G.Murray will parade at 7-30.A.M.and report to O.C."D"Coy.2nd. Labour Battalion at 8.A.M.at Level Crossing of Metre Gange Railway on ALBERT BAPAUME ROAD for work on that road.

In the Field.
1/12/1916.

..................Captain.
Adjutant.8th Battalion Seaforth Highlanders.

Appendix VIII

= 8th SEAFORTH HIGHLANDERS =

= TRAINING PROGRAMME = Week Ending Dec 9th 1916

DATE	MORNING			AFTERNOON	NIGHT	REMARKS
	9am to 10am	11am to 12	12noon to 1pm			
SUNDAY Dec. 3rd.	Church Parade and Baths					
MONDAY Dec. 4th.	Under Coy. Arrangements for MUSKETRY REVETMENT, WIRING, PREVENTATIVE MEASURES against GAS.	PHYSICAL TRAINING and BAYONET FIGHTING	Battalion Drill			Training will be carried out West of the River Groue and South of the AMIENS Road in squads. — E.& O.
TUESDAY Dec. 5th			Battalion at Outpost to Brigade			
WEDNESDAY Dec. 6th			Battalion in the Attack			
THURSDAY Dec. 7th			Battalion Drill			
FRIDAY Dec. 8th			Battalion as Advance Guard to Brigade			
SATURDAY Dec. 9th			Inspection of Billets			

Dec. 2nd 1916

Lloyd W. Innes Captain
Adjutant 8th Seaforth Highlanders

Appendix IX

O.C. All Coys.
Signalling Officer, Pioneer Officer,
Transport Officer & Quartermaster.

1. The Baths in RUE des ILLIEUX are allotted tomorrow as follows:—
   "A" Coy. From 8.A.M. to 9-30.A.M.   "B" Coy From 9-30.A.M. to 11.A.M.
   "C" Coy. "   11.A.M. " 12-30.P.M. "D" Coy " 2.P.M. to 3-30.P.M.

   Headquarters.)
   Transport.   )   From 3-30.P.M. to 5.P.M.
   Pioneers.   )
   Signallers.   )

2. 100 men can bathe an hour.
3. Bathing is compulsory.
4. The Quartermaster will arrange an issue of clean shirts & socks.

George W. Bruce .... Captain.
Adjutant, 8th Bn. Seaforth Highlanders.

2/12/1916.

Appendix X

O.C.All Coys.

In the event of the town being shelled, O.C.Companies must be prepared to receive orders at the shortest notice to evacuate the town.

If such orders are given, movements will probably be ~~made~~ in a North-Easterly direction and must be carried out in silence. On NO account is anyone to leave the town without orders.

3/12/1916.

...................Captain.
Adjutant,6th Bn.Seaforth Highlanders.

Appendix XI

S E C R E T.
O.C. All Coys.

In case the Battalion is ordered to move suddenly, will you please ensure that at least 1 Officer of your Company and 1 Guide per Platoon knows the shortest route from your present billets to the following places:-

HAZEBROUCK-PRADELLE.
QUATRE R....S Gds.
LA MOTSELLE.
BUZINTER.
LE VEN.

The necessary reconnaissances will be made to-morrow.

......................Captain.
Adjutant, 5th Bn. Seaforth Highlanders.

HEADQUARTERS.
Date.................
No.....................
5th (S) Battn. Seaforth Highrs.

SECRET.   15th Division. No. 108/G.a.

44th Infantry Brigade.

      Reference 15th Division No. 108/G.a., para. 10,
    dated 24.11.16.

1.   While the Division is located in its present area Brigades are to be prepared to support Divisions in line.

2.   Possible preliminary moves are for Brigades in ALBERT and BECOURT to relieve Reserve Brigades of Divisions in line in the areas BAZENTIN-le-PETIT and X.21. & 22. Both the 44th and 46th Infantry Brigades to be prepared to carry out either movement.

3.   The 44th Infantry Brigade in ALBERT is also to be prepared to move via LA BOISELLE and POZIERES towards LE SARS if required.

4.   Necessary reconnaissances (in addition to those ordered in para. 10 quoted above) to be carried out.

5.   When the 44th Infantry Brigade finds the three battalions for MAMETZ WOOD the 45th Infantry Brigade is to be prepared to move as in paras. 2 and 3 above.

2nd December 1916.   Sd/ H. KNOX, Lieut. Colonel,
                                   General Staff, 15th Division.

(2)

                                           44th Brigade.
                                           B.M. 4/1.

All Battns. 44th I.B.

      For information. Battalions will make the necessary reconnaissance.

                                                    Captain,
                                               Brigade Major,
3rd Decr. 1916.   44th Infantry Brigade.

Appendix XII

D/4.

O.C.All Coys.
Signalling Officer.
Lewis Gun Officer.
----

1. The following Working Parties of 4 Officers & 200 Other Ranks will be found to-morrow as under:-

    "A"Coy........1 Officer & 50.Men.
    "B"Coy........1 Officer & 50.Men.
    "C"Coy........1 Officer & 50.Men.
    "D"Coy........1 Officer & 50.Men.

    Party will parade under Captain.I.H.S.Jameson & will parade at 7-45.A.M.& report to the Town Major's Office at 8.A.M.
    DRESS:- Clean Fatigue Dress.
    No Tools required.

2. All Training to-morrow will be under Company arrangements as for to-day. Coy's will march to the Training Ground in the order of "B","C","D","A",Signallers & Lewis Gunners.

3. Signallers will train under the Signalling Officer.
    O.C.Coy's will each detail 1 man to report to the Signalling Officer to-morrow for training as Reserve Signallers. These men should,if possible,have previous experience in Signalling.
    O.C.Coy's will also detail 1 man to report to the Signal Officer at 8-45.A.M.for duty as Runners.

4. Lewis Gunners will train under the Lewis Gun Officer.

5. Tunnellers,1 per Platoon,together with the 4 Instructors,& will parade under 2/Lieut.R.V.Cuthbert at 8-45.A.M.tomorrow. The Instructors will remain the same but the remainder should be changed every two days to allow as many men as possible to be trained in this work.

In the Field.
4/12/1916.

............................Captain.
Adjutant.8th Bn.Seaforth Highlanders.

Appendix XIII
44th Brigade.

S E C R E T.

All Battns. 44th I. B.

WARNING ORDER.

1. The 8th Seaforth Highrs., 8/10th Gordon Highrs., and 7th Cameron Highrs. are the battalions selected for work at MAMETZ WOOD.

2. The 9th Black Watch will remain in ALBERT and continue training.

4th Decr. 1916.

Captain,
Brigade Major,
44th Infantry Brigade.

Appendix XIV

44th Brigade.
B.M. 31/16.

All Battns. 44th I.B.

Reference this office B.M. 31/16 dated 1st instant the following additional working party will be found daily by Duty Battalion from to-day up to and including 9th instant :-

    3 Limbers,
    1 N.C.O. and 6 men.
    Tools - 3 picks and 3 Shovels.

Party to report to Camp Commandant, Divisional Headquarters at 8-30 a.m.

Captain,
Brigade Major,
44th Infantry Brigade.

3rd Decr. 1916.

D/5.

Appendix XV

O.C. All Coy's.
Lewis Gunn Officer.
Signalling Officer.
Quartermaster.
Transport Officer.

1. The following Working Parties will be found to-morrow as under:-

   (a) 4 Officers & 200 men:-   "B"Coy. 2 Officers & 70 men.
                                "C"Coy. 1 Officer & 65 men.
                                "D"Coy. 1 Officer & 65 men.
   This party will parade under Captain A.W.Turnbull at 7-40.A.M.
   & will report to O.C."D"Coy 2nd Labour Battalion at 8.A.M.
   at the Level Crossing of Metre Gange Railway on ALBERT
   BAPAUME ROAD for work on that road.
   Dress :- Clean Fatigue Dress. No Tools required.

   (b) 1 Officer & 40.Other Ranks of "A"Coy to take over Guard
   on German Prisoners at E.3.a.

   This party will parade at 6-45.A.M.& report at E.3.a at
   7-30 A.M.   They will not be releived till 7_30.A.M.on
   December,7th.   The Quartermaster will arrange for Blankets
   & Rations etc to be transported to them.
   Dress:-Skeleton Equipment.

   (c) 1 N.C.O & 20 Other Ranks to be found by Battn Signallers.

   This Party will parade at Bn Hd Qrs at 9-30.A.M.
   Dress:- Clean Fatigue Dress.
   20 Shovels will be drawn from the Quartermaster Stores.

   (d) 1 NC.O & 6 men of "A"Coy.

   This Party will parade at 8.A.M.and report to Camp Commandant,
   15th Divisional Headquarters at 8-30.A.M.
   The Transport Officer will detail 3 Limbers to accompany
   this party.
   Dress :- Clean Fatigue Dress.
   Tools required:-3.Picks & 3 Shovels. These will be drawn
   from the Quartermaster Stores.

2. Parties (a) & (b) will carry haversack rations.

3. Tunnellers will carry on training to-morrow as usual under
   2/Lt R.V.Cuthbert.

In the Field.
5/12/1916.
...................Captain.
Adjutant.8th Bn.Seaforth Highlanders.

Duplicate W.D.
Appendix XVI

S E C R E T.   COPY No. 2

44TH INFANTRY BRIGADE OPERATION ORDER No. 121.

Tuesday 5th Decr. 1916.

Reference Map :
ALBERT Combined Sheet. 1/40,000

1. Reliefs in accordance with attached Table will take place on the 7th December.

2. Transport will accompany units with such articles as may be required in Camp.
Further orders will be issued as to its disposal and also that of articles not taken to Camp.

3. During all movements distances of 200 yards will be maintained between battalions and distances of 100 yards between platoons or parties of equivalent road space.

4. Battalions will send advanced parties at 9 a.m., 7th December, to ascertain the exact work being carried out by the battalions they relieve.

5. Working parties will work from 7 a.m. to 4 p.m. daily, commencing on the 8th December.

6. The 9th Black Watch will be duty battalion on the 7th December.

7. Completion of reliefs will be reported to Brigade Headquarters.

8. Brigade Headquarters will remain at ALBERT.

                                                                 Captain,
                                                        Brigade Major,
Issued through   44th Infantry Brigade.
  Signals.

      Copy No. 1. 9th Black Watch.
               2. 8th Seaforth Hrs.
               3. 8/10th Gordon Hrs.
               4. 7th Cameron Hrs.
               5. 44th M. G. Company.
               6. 44th T. M. Battery.
               7. H.Q., 15th Division.
               8. 45th Inf. Bde.
               9. 46th Inf. Bde.
             10. Bde. Transport Officer.
             11. Bde. Supply Officer.
             12. Bde. Signal Officer.
             13. No. 2 Coy. Train.
             14. Staff Captain.
             15. War Diary.
             16. File.

RELIEF TABLE to accompany 11th Infantry Brigade Operation Order No.121 d/5.12.18.

Relieving Units.	Units being relieved.	Starting Point.	Time.	Route.	Remarks.
8/10th Gordon Hrs.	11th A. & S. Hrs.	BELLEVUE FARM E.5.c.7.6.	P.M. 1-20	ALBERT – FRICOURT to Camps about X.23.Central.	
8th Seaforth Hrs.	13th Royal Scots.		2- 0		Billets vacated by 8th Seaforth Hrs. will be taken over by 6th Cameron Hrs.
7th Cameron Hrs.	6/7th R. S. Fusrs.		2-30		

attach app XVI

SECRET.

44th Brigade.

Addendum No. 1 to 44th Inf. Bde. Operation Order No.121
dated 5th December 1916.

1. Reference Relief Table. Starting Point will be at road junction on main ALBERT - BAPAUME Road at W.29.b.7.5.

2. Time and order of marching remains unchanged.

3. Transport wagons are not allowed to go beyond CONTALMAISON. From thence baggage must be carried to Camps.

4. Battalion transport will be kept in the outskirts of ALBERT and not up at the Camps.

Captain,
Brigade Major,
44th Infantry Brigade.

6th Decr. 1916.

Copy to All Units 44th I.B.
45th Inf. Bde.
H.Q., 15th Division.

Attach App XVI

44th Brigade.
S.C. 17/106

All Units 44th Inf. Bde.

     Units will retain their present Q.M.Stores in ALBERT during the period the Division is in Reserve.

     When the Division moves into the forward area the Stores in RUE d'AUSSY will be taken over.

     The Units of the 45th Brigade arriving in ALBERT will not take over the Q.M.Stores at present occupied by us as others have been allotted them.

                                            Captain,
                                       Staff Captain,
6th December 1916.   44th Infantry Brigade.

SECRET

Appendix XVII
10

OPERATION ORDER No 45.
by
Lt. Col. N. A. Thomson, D.S.O.
Commdg. 8th Seaforth High'rs —

Ref. Map.   Dec. 6th/16
1/40,000. ALBERT COMBINED SHEET:—

1. The Battalion will march to-morrow to camp at X.23. Central, as follows, to relieve 13th Battn. The Royal Scots.
   STARTING POINT — FORKED ROADS next Sergeant's Mess
   TIME .... — 1.40 p.m.
   ORDER of MARCH — "C", "D", "A" and "B" Coys.
   ROUTE .... — Road Junction on main ALBERT-BAPAUME ROAD, at W.29.b.7.5, W.29.d, E.5.Central, to ALBERT-FRICOURT Road MAMETZ-CONTALMAISON ROAD to camp at X.23. Central.
   DRESS .... — Full Marching Order.
   All movements will be by ½ Coys. at 100 yds. interval.

2. An advanced party of 1 officer per Coy. and 2 men per platoon will parade outside Battalion H.Q. at 9 a.m. under 2/Lieut. G.G. Blackwood and proceed to the Camp to take over and ascertain the exact work being carried out by the Battalion being relieved.

3. All Blankets will be rolled in bundles of 10,- labelled and taken to the Quartermasters Stores by 10 a.m. to-morrow:-
   Officers valises will be reduced to 35 lbs. and taken to Quartermasters Stores by 12. noon. Any surplus to the above weight will be left behind and be taken to Quartermaster's Stores by 11.30 a.m.
   Mess Boxes will be collected at 1.30 p.m.

4. Cookers, water-carts, medical cart and mess cart will follow 100 yds. in rear of the last platoon of "B" Coy.
   Dinners to-morrow will be at 12.15 p.m.

5. A rear party of 4 men per Coy. and 4 from H.Q., will remain behind under an officer to be detailed by O.C "C" Coy. who will report to the Adjutant for instructions.

George W. Duncan.
Capt.
Adjutant, 8th Seaforth Highlanders.

DISTRIBUTION
COPY N° 1. O.C "A" Coy.   6. Transport Officer
        2. O.C "B" Coy.   7. Quartermaster.
        3. O.C "C" Coy.   8. Lewis Gun Officer.
        4. O.C "D" Coy.   9. War Diary.
        5. 2nd in Command.   10. File.

Secret
Urgent.

Appendix XVIII

HEADQUARTERS
7 DEC 1916
No. BM 642
44th Inf...

O.C.
8" Seaforth

With reference to attached order, please detail a half company (Men must not be selected) to carry out test.

The test will probably take place in the vicinity of MAMETZ WOOD about 11 am 8th inst.

Please note men must be in full fighting order.

Orders as to rendezvous will be issued later.

Later. Rendezvous S 2 c 8 1 just west of Martinpuich – Bazentin Road at 11.30 am 8th inst.

Waugh. Captain,
Bde. Major
44th Infy Bde.

7/11/16.

15th Division No. 107/G.a.

Appendix XVIII

44th Inf. Bde.

1.   Would you please carry out a test on the 8th inst., if possible :-

Object. To ascertain as far as is possible the rate at which troops can advance under present weather conditions over ground much broken by shell fire.

2.   It is suggested that the test be carried out by a few men in fighting order at some point where the ground is well broken.

Men must be timed over an advance of 300 yards. Distance covered in each minute to be reported. Condition of men at end of advance to be reported on.

3.   Will you please say time and place you can carry out the test.

                                    Sd/ E. DUNCOMBE, Captain,
                                         for Lieut. Colonel,
7th Decr. 1916.   General Staff 15th Division.

44th Brigade.
B.M. 33.

Appendix XIX

War Diary

44th Infantry Brigade.

"Each Brigade will find the following parties for instructional work with 179th Tunnelling Co. R.E. AAA
(a) 1 officer and 5 O.R. to report to O.C. Detachment 179th Tunnelling Co. R.E. MARTINPUICH at M.27.c.3.½ on the afternoon of the 7th Party to take 2 days Rations. AAA
(b) 3 officers and 30 O.R. to work in 3 reliefs reporting to representative of 179th Tunnelling Co. R.E. at S.3.A. at 8 a.m., 4 p.m. and 12 midnight commencing at 8 a.m. on the 8th instant AAA *   *   *   AAA
All parties will rejoin Brigades when the Division moves into the line AAA

15th Division."

All Battns. 44th I.B.
O.C. 179th (T) Coy. R.E. - for information.

....

Reference above 15th Divisional wire.

1.　　O.C., 9th Black Watch will find party of 1 Officer and 5 Other Ranks, as in (a) above.

2.　　Parties for (b) will be found as follows :-

(1) 8th Seaforth Hrs.　1 Off. 10 O.R.　To report at 8 a.m.

(2) 8/10th Gordon Hrs.　1 Off. 10 O.R.　To report at 4 p.m.

(3) 7th Cameron Hrs.　1 Off. 10 O.R.　To report at 12 Mdnt.

Captain,
Brigade Major,
44th Infantry Brigade.

6th Decr. 1916.

44th Brigade.
B.M. 33.

O. C., 8th Seaforth Hrs.,
     8/10th Gordon Hrs.,
     7th Cameron Hrs.
  179th (T) Coy. R.E. - for information.

I. With reference to this office B.M. 33 of 6th Decr., para. 2.

1. Parties for (b) will be found as follows :-

    7th & 8th Decr.   8th Seaforth Hrs.

    9th & 10th "   8/10th Gordon Hrs.

    11th & 12th "   7th Cameron Hrs.

2. Each battalion will detail 3 officers and 30 men to work in 3 reliefs -

(i)   1 Off. and 10 O.R. to report at 8 a.m. daily

(ii)   1 "   " 10 "   " "   " 4 p.m. "

(iii) 1 "   " 10 "   " "   " 12 Midnight.

3. It has been ascertained from 179th (T) Coy. R.E. that these men will only be employed in the actual digging and fitting of timbers. As it is all work under-ground it is immaterial whether it is carried out in daylight or not.

4. It is understood that the shafts have been finished and that the work on the construction of the chambers is now being carried out.

                                        Captain,
                                   Brigade Major,
7th December 1916.   44th Infantry Brigade.

Appendix XX.

SECRET.   Copy No. 2

44th Infantry Brigade Operation Order No.122.

Reference.-   Thursday 14th Dec., 1916.
ALBERT (Combined Sheet). 1/40,000.

1. The 15th Division (less Artillery) will relieve the 48th Division (less Artillery) in the Left Sector III Corps on the 14th/15th and 16th December.

2. Reliefs on the 16th December of the 44th Infantry Brigade will take place in accordance with the attached relief table. (& 45 I Bde)

3. During all movements distances of 100 yards will be maintained between platoons and equivalent units.

4. Transport will march in rear of units and will be accommodated at CHAPES SPUR. Each unit will take over the same standings as it occupied when the brigade was last in the line.
Entrance to Transport Lines is by Cross Roads at X.13.d.3.0.

5. All units will send advanced parties to the H.Qrs. of units they relieve by 10 A.M. on the 16th December.
Units being relieved are also sending advanced parties at the same hour.

6. The 9th Black Watch, 44 M.G.Coy., and 44 T.M.Battery will leave rear parties to hand over their billets to incoming units.

7. Receipts will be taken for all camp equipment handed over at MAMETZ CAMP, and sent to Brigade Headquarters by 10 A.M. on the 17th December.

8. Receipts will be given for all hut equipment, stores etc. taken over in the SHELTER WOOD - SCOYS REDOUBT area.

9. The 8th Seaforth Highlanders, 8/10th Gordons, and 7th Cameron's working parties will carry out their usual work on the 16th and then proceed direct to their new area allotted in the attached Relief Table.
Battalions will give relieving battalions full details of work being carried out, and rendezvous for the 17th December.

10. Working parties from 17th December inclusive will be found by the 44th Infantry Brigade in accordance with the attached addendum.

11. Brigade Headquarters will close at ALBERT at 9-30 A.M. and open simultaneously at SHELTER WOOD H.Qrs.

Issued through   Captain,
Signals.   Brigade Major,
3 A.M. 15th Decbr, 1916, to :-   44th Infantry Brigade.
Copy No. 1. 9th Black Watch.   2. 8th Seaforths.
        3. 8/10th Gordons.   4. 7th Camerons.
        5. 44 M.G.Coy.   6. 44 T.M.Battery.
        7. 15th Div.   8. 144th Inf. Bde.
        9. 45th Inf. Bde.   10. 46th Inf. Bde.
       11. 48th Div.Arty.   12. Town Major, ALBERT.
       13. Bde.Supply Officer.   14. Bde.Transport Offcr.
       15. No.2 Coy.Train.   16. Bde.Signalling Offcr.
       17. Staff Capt.   18 A.P.M.,15th Div.
       19 War Diary.   20. File.

March Table of reliefs on 16th December, 1916, issued with
4th Infantry Brigade Operation Order No.122 dated 14th December, 1916.

Relieving unit.	Unit being relieved.	Starting Point.	Time.	Route.	Units taking over from 4th Inf.Bde.Units.
8/10th Gordons. (MAMETZ CAMP NORTH).	4th Gloucesters. (SCOTS REDOUBT SOUTH).	Camp.	P.M. 12-30	Most convenient.	4th Gloucesters.
8th Seaforths. (MAMETZ CAMP SOUTH).	6th Gloucesters. (SHELTER WOOD NORTH).	Camp.	1-30	- do -	6th Gloucesters.
7th Camerons. (MAMETZ CAMP WEST).	8th Worcesters. (SCOTS REDOUBT NORTH).	Camp.	2-30	- do -	8th Worcesters.
9th Black Watch. (ALBERT).	13th Royal Scots. (SHELTER WOOD SOUTH).	Cross Roads BELLEVUE FARM. E.5.c.7.6.	A.M. 9-0	ALBERT - FRICOURT.	7th Worcesters.
44 M.G.Coy. (ALBERT).	15th M.G.Coy. (SHELTER WOOD. X.21.d.)	- do -	9-30	- do -	14th M.G.Coy.
44 T.M.Battery. (ALBERT).	15th T.M.Battery. (SHELTER WOOD. X.21.d.)	- do -	9-40	- do -	14th T.M.Battery.

ADDENDUM No.1 TO 44TH INFANTRY BRIGADE OPERATION ORDER No.122.
List of Working Parties to be found by 44th Infantry Brigade when in the line.

Battalion Finding party.	Number.			To	To Report Place.	Time.	Work.	Remarks.
	Off.	N.C.Os.	Men.					
9th Black Watch	1.	1.	20.	180th Tunnelling Coy.	X.16.b.5.5.	6 P.M. 16th inst.	Dugouts in front line & Corps line.	This will be a permanent party and will remain with the Tunnelling Coy. at X.16.b.5.5. Parties to be rationed for 16th instant by Battalions.
8th Seaforths.	-	1.	20.					
8/10th Gordons.	-	1.	14.	179th Tunnelling Coy.	MARTINPUICH.	6 P.M. 16th inst.	Dugouts in Intermediate Line.	This will be a permanent party and will remain with the Tunnelling Coy in MARTINPUICH (exact place will be notified later). Party to be rationed for 17th inst. by battalion.
7th Camerons.	-	1.	14.	R.E. N.C.O. in charge of Store.	X.16.b.2.4.	6 P.M. 16th inst.	R.E.Stores. CONTALMAISON VILLA Road.	This will be a permanent party and will remain with the R.E. at X.16.b.2.4.
Duty Battalion.	1.	2.	40.	5th Sussex Regt. Pioneers.	X.16.b.2.4.	8-30 A.M.		This will be found by the Brigade in reserve, commencing on 17th instant. Instructions will be issued daily.

War Diary

"C" Form (Original).
MESSAGES AND SIGNALS.

Army Form C. 2123.

Prefix SM	Code ADS	Words 48	Received From HR	Sent, or sent out	Office Stamp
Charges to collect			By WW	At ... m. To ... By	✓
Service Instructions ZDD					

Handed in at .... 44 B Office 1.22 P.m. Received 1.35 P.m.

TO — 8th Seaforth Hrs

Sender's Number	Day of Month	In reply to Number	AAA
BM 65	15	—	

Ref addendum 1 to 44th Inf Bde OO.122 AAA Parties for work with 180th (T) Coy will now be rationed to 17th inst. AAA Arrange AAA addsd Battns concerned/replid 180th (T) Coy and 15th Devn.

WRB

FROM PLACE & TIME — 44th Inf Bde 12.15 PM

OPERATION ORDERS No. 46
by
Lieut. Col. N. H. Thomson, D.S.O.
Commdg. 8th Battn. Seaforth Highlanders Appendix XXI

Ref. Map. 1/40,000 ALBERT.
— Dec. 15th 1914

1. The Battalion will move to-morrow to Huts at SHELTER WOOD – South – X.22.C. to relieve the 13th Battn. The Royal Scots.
All Working Parties will cease at 12 noon.
ORDER OF MARCH A, B, C and D Coys., Sigs. & Runners, Police.

   TIME   First Coy. will move off at 12.45 p.m.
   ROUTE   Direct across country.
   DRESS   Full Marching Order.

   All movement to be by ½ Coys. at 5 mins. interval.
   All Lewis Guns will move at 1 p.m. under 2/Lieut. C. Forrest, who will arrange with the Transport Officer for assistance.

2. Each Coy. will clear one tent and have all their blankets rolled in bundles of 10 and stacked in it by 7 a.m.

3. A carrying party of 25 men per Coy. under Coy. S.M's will be detailed as a carrying party. This party will include 1 Lewis Gun team from each Coy.
Of this party, 23 men per Coy., in clean fatigue dress, will parade at their Blanket Tents at 8 a.m. and will be under the direction of the Qr.Mr. They will proceed to SHELTER WOOD. SOUTH where they will stack their blankets in their Coy. Lines. 1 N.C.O. and 1 man per Coy. in full marching order, with haversack Rations will report to the Qr.Mr. at 8 a.m. for instructions.
Officers baggage will be ready to be collected at 9.30 a.m.

4. The Transport Officer will arrange to have 3 Limbers, Pack Ponies and Mules at the Camp at 9.30 a.m. to assist the Transport of supplies etc. and to assist with the Lewis Gun hand carts.
Coy. Cookers will leave this Camp at 11 AM and report to the Qr. Master on arrival at SHELTER WOOD SOUTH. Dinner, to-morrow, will be at 2 p.m. at SHELTER WOOD SOUTH.

5. Coys. will each arrange to vacate and clear 2 tents on the North flank of their Coy. Lines by 9 a.m. to enable the incoming Battn. to stack their stores.

2/Lieut.
Asst. Adjutant 8th Seaforth Highlanders

War Diary Appendix XXII

44th Brigade.
S.G. 11/46.

All Battns. 44th I. B.
Bde. Transport Officer.
44th M. G. Company.

    Owing to the majority of units' transport being on the road to-morrow, the relief of the First Line Transport will take place on 17th instant. The 144th Brigade First Line Transport will be clear by Noon.

    Arrangements have been made to this effect between the two Transport Officers concerned. Units, including Machine Gun Company, will take up their Standings on CHAPES SPUR and Battalions will occupy the same lines as before.

H. Parole Captain,
for Staff Captain,
44th Infantry Brigade.

15th Decr. 1916.

Appendix XXIII
Working Party

duty bttn.
8th Seaforths —

WORKING PARTY.

11th Brigade.

No. of Officers. 3

No. of Men. 4 N.C.O. 160 men

Date. 17

Time. 8.30 a.m.

Rendez-vous LOMBARD CIRCUS S.14.B.1.8

To report to 5th Sussex Regt (Pioneers)

Nature of work ?

Tools. nil Picks. Shovels.

Haversack Rations required.

Date. 16 Dec 1915.
Time. 3-7pm

W Ward Captain,
Brigade Major,
11th Infantry Brigade.

Appendix XXIV

SECRET.   Copy No. 2

44th Infantry Brigade Operation Order No.123.

                              Monday, 18th Decbr., 1916.

1. The 44th Infantry Brigade will relieve the 45th Infantry Brigade in the line on the 19th December in accordance with Relief Table shown on other side.

2. Vickers guns in the line will be relieved, but Stokes Mortars will be handed over in position.

3. During all movements as far as the trench boards distances of 100 yards will be maintained between platoons and equivalent units.

4. The 8/10th Gordon Highrs. and 9th Seaforths will take over 100% tools on relief. These will be handed over at positions of pickets and supports.

5. All trench stores will be taken over and receipts given ~~taken~~. Combined returns to reach Brigade Headquarters by 5 P.M. 21st instant.

6. On completion of relief two sections 91st Field Coy. R.E., will come under the orders of the 44th Infantry Brigade.

7. Completion of relief to be reported to Brigade Headquarters (M.32.a.2½.2.) by wire.

Brigade Headquarters will close and open simultaneously at 3 P.M.

Issued   Captain,
Through Signals.   Brigade Major,
 4 P.M.   44th Infantry Brigade.

Copies to :-
  No. 1. 9th Black Watch.
      2. 8th Seaforths.
      3. 8/10th Gordons.
      4. 7th Camerons.
      5. 44 M.G.Coy.
      6. 44 T.M.Bty.
      7. 15th Div.
      8. 45th Inf. Bde.
      9. 46th Inf. Bde.
     10. 153rd Inf. Bde.
     11. Left Group Arty.
     12. Supply Offer. 44th Bde.
     13. No. 2 Coy. Train.
     14. Bde. Transport Officer.
     15. Bde. Bombing Officer.
     16. Bde. Signals.
     17. Staff Capt.
     18. War Diary.
     19 File.

TABLE TO ACCOMPANY 44TH INFANTRY BRIGADE OPERATION ORDER No. 123, d/18-12-16.

Relieving Units In order of relief.	Units being relieved.	GUIDES.	Time & Place.	Route.	Remarks.
7th Camerons. (SCOTS REDOUBT N.)	6th Cameron Highrs. (ACID DROP SOUTH) Reserve.	Guides – Nil. Relief to commence at 1-15 P.M.		Most convenient	Advanced parties to take over Camp from 6th Camerons on morning 19th. Bn.H.Q. ACID DROP SOUTH.
9th Black Watch. (SHELTER WOOD N.)	13th Royal Scots. (VILLA CAMP – 2nd Support).	Guides – Nil. Relief to commence at 2 P.M.		– do –	Advanced parties to take over camp from 13th R.Scots. Bn. H.Q. VILLA CAMP.
44 M.G.Coy. (SHELTER WOOD).	45 M.G.Coy. H.Q. MILL CUTTING. M.27.c.	Guides 1 per gun in line and 1 for Coy.H.Q. CONTALMAISON VILLA 3-30 P.M.		Under arrangements between C.Os. concerned.	44 M.G.Coy. not to leave camp before 2-30 P.M. H.Q. M.27.c.
44 T.M.Battery.	45 T.M.Battery. MIDDLE WOOD.	Guides – 1 per Mortar in line. MIDDLE WOOD, 3-30 P.M.		– do –	44 T.M.Bty not to leave camp before 2-45 P.M. On completion of relief T.M.Bty. will open H.Qrs. at VILLA WOOD.
8/10th Gordons. (SCOTS REDOUBT S.)	11th A.& S.Hrs. (Front line).	1 per platoon, 1 Bn. H.Q. CONTALMAISON VILLA 4 P.M.		– do –	Bn. H.Qrs. – M.21.d.9.6.
8th Seaforths. (SHELTER WOOD S.)	6/7th R.S.F. (1st Support).			– do –	Bn. H.Qrs. – M.21.d.3.0.

Appendix XXV

SECRET.   OPERATION   ORDER   No. 47.
by
Lieut. Col. N.A. Thomson, D.S.O.,
Commdg 8th. Bn. Seaforth Highlanders.
-:-

Reference Map 15th. Div. No.17 B.

1. The Battalion will relieve the 6/7th. Bn. R.S.F. in Support to-morrow as follows:-
    "A" Coy. will relieve "A" Coy. R.S.F. in 26th. AVENUE.
    "C" Coy. will relieve "C" Coy. R.S.F. in 26th. AVENUE.
    "B" Coy. will relieve "B" Coy. R.S.F. in MARTINPUICH.
    "D" Coy. will relieve "D" Coy. R.S.F. in MARTINPUICH.
   Battalion H.Q. will move to Point M.21.d.3.0.
   During all movements distances of 100 yards will be maintained between Platoons and equivalent units.
   DRESS. Trench Order. Gum Boots will be carried and will not be worn until arrival in the trenches.

2. Guides (1 per platoon and 1 from Bn. H.Q.) will meet at CONTALMAISON VILLA at 4 p.m.

3. One Officer per Coy., the a/B.S.M., the Signalling Sgt. and one N.C.O. per platoon to go as an advance party to be in new positions at 2.p.m to take over trench stores. The Battalion will take over 100 % tools on relief.
   This advance party will make itself acquainted with the shortest route from their Coy. Lines to the Front Line in case their Coys. are required to re-inforce.

4. All blankets to be rolled in bundles of 10 and deposited in Coy. Q.M. Stores by 10 a.m.
   All Officers Valises, surplus kit, and surplus Mess material to be in Battn. Q.M. Stores by 12 noon.

5. Bombs, Ammunition and Sand-bags will be issued at Battn. Q.M. Stores as follows:-
    "A" Coy. ....12 noon.
    "B" Coy. ....12.15 p.m.
    "C" Coy. ....12.30 p.m.
    "D" Coy. ....12.45 p.m.
   O.s C. Coys. will report when the issues are complete.

6. Separate Ration parties will meet rations to-morrow at 5 p.m. in MARTINPUICH on the Light Railway at about Point M.32.a.2½.2.
   Rations will be loaded at VILLA STATION by train leaving there at 4.30 p.m.

7. One Reserve Lewis Gun Team per Coy. in full Marching Order with 2 blankets per man, under the Lewis Gun Sgt., will parade at 1.30 p.m. and will report to the Adjutant 7th. Bn. Cameron Highrs. at ACID DROP SOUTH. This party will be rationed by the Battalion in Reserve from the 22nd. inst inclusive.

8. O.sC. Coy.s. will report to Battalion H.Q. when relief is complete.

...........................2/Lieut.,
a/Adjutant 8th. Battalion Seaforth Highlanders.

Distribution.
Copy. No. 1 O.C. "A" Coy.   6. Signalling Officer.
         2. O.C. "B" Coy.   7. 2/Lieut. J.H.Poss
         3. O.C. "C" Coy.   8. Quartermaster.
         4. O.C. "D" Coy.   9. War Diary.
         5. Transport Officer. 10. File.

Issued through Signals at.....................12.15 p.m.

-------------- oOo --------------

OC 8th Seaforth Highrs – for information. Appendix XXVI

Secret

Operation Orders No. 2.

(1) The Battn will be relieved tomorrow (19th) by the 8th Seaforth Highrs.

(2) Guides, 1 per platoon & 1 for HQ will be at D Coy HQ, MARTINPUICH, at 3 PM. 2/Lieut J.K. Couper will take charge of them and will be at CONTALMAISON VILLA by 4.30 PM.

(3) The probable relief is A coy SH relieves A RSF & so on.

(4) On relief Battn will move to camp in SHELTER WOOD SOUTH.

(5) All tools will be dumped near Coy HQ and handed over in trench stores – receipts for trench stores will be handed in at Orderly Room by 10 am 20th inst.

(6) Completion of relief to be reported by wire to Battn HQ.

(7) An advance party of 1 NCO and 2 men per coy, and L/Cpl Logan from HQ will be at D coy HQ at 10 am. 2/Lt. Buchan "C" coy, will take charge. They will proceed to SHELTER WOOD SOUTH and take over camp from 8th Seaforths.

(8) Hot tea will be served on arrival in camp in the evening.

(9) Acknowledge.

18-12-16.

W Pettigrew
Adj
6/7 RSF

War Diary

Appendix XXVII

44th Brigade M.R.869/1.

SECRET.

All units 44th Inf. Bde.
81st Field Coy. R.E.
15th Division. For information.

The following revised table shows how the battalion reliefs will probably be carried out when the 44th Infantry Brigade goes into the left section in relief of the 45th Inf.Bde. on the 19th/20th Decbr.

	19th.	20th.	21st.	22nd.	23rd.	24th.	25th.	26th.	27th.
"A" Battn. 8/10th Gordons.									
"B" Battn. 9th Seaforths.									
"C" Battn. 9th Black Watch.									
"D" Battn. 7th Camerons.									

▮ battalion in Front Line.

▮ battalion in Support.

▮ battalion in 2nd Support.

▮ battalion in Reserve.

19-12-15.

Captain,
Brigade Major,
44th Infantry Brigade.

SECRET.   Copy No. 2

44th Infantry Brigade Operation Order No. 124.

20-12-16.

1. The following reliefs will take place to-morrow, the 21st/22nd December.

2. The 8th Seaforth Highrs. will relieve the 8/10th Gordon Highrs. in the left sub-section of the front line system.
   Relief to commence at 5 P.M.
   Route CHALK WALK.

3. The 7th Cameron Highrs. will relieve the 8/10th Gordon Highrs in the right sub-section of the front line system.
   The 7th Camerons will not pass over the HIGH WOOD - POZIERES RIDGE before 4 P.M.

4. On relief the 8/10th Gordons will move into reserve in ACID DROP SOUTH. They will send an advanced party by 2 P.M. to take over all camp equipment.

5. The 9th Black Watch will stand fast.

6. All arrangements will be made direct between Officers Commanding concerned.

7. The 7th Camerons will arrange to take over 100% tools from the 8/10th Gordons.

8. The right and left front battalions will have their companies distributed approximately in accordance with map B.M.691 issued 20th December.

9. Completion of relief will be reported by wire to Brigade Headquarters.

Issued
through Signals.
11-30 P.M.

                                            Captain,
                                         Brigade Major,
                                      44th Infantry Brigade.

        Copy No. 1. 9th Black Watch.
                 2. 8th Seaforths.
                 3. 8/10th Gordons.
                 4. 7th Camerons.
                 5. 44 M.G.Coy.
                 6. 44 T.M.Battery.
                 7. 15th Division.
                 8. 46th Inf. Bde.
                 9. 154th Inf. Bde.
                10. War Diary.
                11. File.

SECRET

Appendix XXIX War Diary No 9

OPERATION ORDER No 48
by
Lieut. Col. N.A. Thomson D.S.O.
Commdg. 8th Battn. Seaforth Hdrs.   21/12/16

(1) The Battn. will relieve the 8/10th Gordons in the left section of the firing line tonight.

(2) "D" Coy. will relieve "D" Coy 8/10th Gordons in the front line. One H.Q. Lewis Gun Team will move with "D" Coy. One platoon of "C" Coy will relieve 1 platoon of "A" Coy 8/10th Gordons on the left flank of the line. The remaining 3 platoons will relieve the remaining 3 platoons 8/10th Gordons in Battn. Support.

(3) Guides, 1 per platoon, from D & A Coys. 8/10th Gordons will meet platoons at junction of GILBERT ALLEY and ALBERT - BAPAUME RD. at 6 p.m.

(4) RATIONS "D" & "C" Coys. will each carry a full days rations with them.

(5) TOOLS 100% will be carried.

(6) "A" Coy. will move into an area S.W. of Bde. H.Q. and "B" Coy. into an area in vicinity of 70th AVENUE & GUN-PIT-TRENCH. Both areas to be pointed out by the Staff Capt. 44th Inf. Bde.

(7) "C" & "D" Coys. will dump their Gum Boots at the Drying Shed in MARTINPUICH.

(8) Relief, when complete, will be reported by wire to Battn. H.Q. by O's C. Coys.

21/12/16   2/Lt.
                    ⅔ Adjutant 8th Seaforth Hdrs

Copy No 1 OC A Coy   6 Qr. Mr.
        2 OC B Coy   7 Trans. Officer
        3 OC C Coy   8 } War Diary
        4 OC D Coy   9 }
        5 Sigs. Officer   10 FILE

"A" Form. Army Form C. 2121.
MESSAGES AND SIGNALS

This message is on a/c of:
Appx
(Signature of "Franking Officer.")

From XXX

TO: O C A, B, C, D Coys
       OC 7th S[eaforths]?

Sender's Number: GH/39
Day of Month: 21st
AAA

1. Battn. will be relieved in the line on night 21/22.

2. 7th Camerons (2 Coys) relieve 2 right Coys (B & C) 8/10 Gordons

3. 8th Seaforths (2 Coys) relieve 2 left Coys (D & A) 8/10 Gordons

4. Battn. on relief will move into Camp at ACID DROP COPSE X.17.C.

5. No limbers are being provided for transport L. Guns + ammn, water-tins (empty) and Battn. property will be distributed amongst the men, and carried to Camp.

6. Platoons on relief will move out independently & proceed direct to Camp.

(T.P.T.O)

"A" Form.
MESSAGES AND SIGNALS
Army Form C. 2121.

TO		2		

* Sender's Number | Day of Month | In reply to Number | **AAA**

7. 5/th All tools will be handed over to 7/th Camerons. They will be collected for handing over at B, C Coys H.Q. respectively.

8. D Coy. Seaforths relieves D Coy Gordons
   C   "   "   A   "   "
   Guides - 1 per platoon for above will be at Junction of GILBERT ALLEY & BAPAUME ROAD at 6 p.m. 21st inst. aaa

9. C B Coy Camerons relieves B Coy Gordons O C C Coy will send 4 guides to meet C Coy Camerons at MARTINPUICH JUNCTION (Duckboard fork) at 4.30 p.m. 21st inst aaa. O.C. B Coy Gordons will have 4 guides (1 per platoon) at the Junction of GILBERT ALLEY and BAPAUME ROAD at 6 p.m.

From
Place
Time

"A" Form.
MESSAGES AND SIGNALS
Army Form C. 2121.

TO		3	

9. cont^d. C Coys (Gordons) guides will lead C Coy Camerons up CHALK WALK to Junction of GILBERT ALLEY and BAPAUME R^d where they will hand them over to B Coy (Gordons) guides who will conduct them to front line.

C. Coys (Gordons) guides may then move out independently.

10. Support Coy (Camerons) relieves C Coy (Gordons) Guides 1 per platoon from C Coy (Gordons) will be at MARTINPUICH JUNCTION at 4-30 p.m. They will conduct Support Coy (Camerons) via LE SARS WALK to O.G.1. & relieving C Coy (Gordons)

11. One guide from H.Q^{rs} for Cameron H.Q^{rs} will be at MARTINPUICH Junction at 4.30 p.m. to conduct them via LE SARS WALK to H.Q^{rs}.

| "A" Form. | Army Form C. 2121. |
| MESSAGES AND SIGNALS | No. of Message............ |

Day of Month: 21st

4

NOTE:— Western branch Duckboard Walk is known as "CHALK WALK". Eastern Branch as "LE SARS WALK." Reliable Guides must be sent in each case.

12. Receipts for all Trench Stores handed over will be rendered to Orderly Room by noon 22nd inst.

13. Relief complete to be reported to Battn. HQrs by wire.

Crawford — Lieut + Adjt.
8/10th Gordon Highrs

~~SECRET~~

OPERATION ORDER. No 49   No 1
Lieut Col. N. A. Thomson D.S.O.
Commdg. 8th Seaforth Hrs – Dec 22nd 1916

(1) "A" Coy. will relieve "D" Coy. in the front line, as under, tonight.

(2) "D" Coy. will continue work from dusk till 10 p.m. (wiring)

(3) Guides will meet at 9 p.m. at junction of BAPAUME ROAD with GILBERT ALLEY. Guides will be one per platoon.

(4) The H.Q. Lewis Gun Team attached to "D" Coy. will not be relieved. It will remain in position and will be attached to "A" Coy. for duty. Rations for this Team will be drawn and taken up by "A" Coy.

(5) "A" Coy. will carry on the man one days rations in addition to the "Iron Ration." Solidified alcohol will be carefully distributed to enable men on detached posts to cook during their tour of duty.

(6) "A" Coy. will dump their tools before leaving and will take over 100% tools from "D" Coy.

(7) Capt. Thornton will meet Capt. Jameson at the latter's H. Qrs. at 7 p.m. and will overlook the ground and will make himself acquainted with the dispositions of the Company and the work on hand. Capt. Thornton will take with him such stuff as he may require.

(8) "A" Coy. will continue work in the Coy. area after the relief is complete. Special attention is

(8) cont.
to be paid to "wiring" intermediate ground between picquets

(9) Relief when complete to be reported to Battn. HQrs. by wire.

/Adjutant 8' Seaforth Hrs 7hr.

Distribution
Copy No. 1 OC A Coy
     2 OC B Coy
     3 OC C Coy
     4 OC D Coy
     5 Sig. officer
     6 QMr.
     7 } War Diary
     8 }
     9 File.

After Order

The picquet found by "C" Coy. west of the Chalk Pit, will be relieved under Coy. arrangements.

"A" Coy. will draw & carry up "C" Coys. rations, dumping them at "C" Coy. H. Qrs. M.15.c.8.6, en route.

SECRET.　　　　　　　　　　　　　　Copy No. 2

44th Infantry Brigade Operation Order No. 125.
_____

Friday, 22nd Decbr., 1916.

1. The following reliefs will take place to-morrow the 23rd/24th December.

2. The 9th Black Watch will relieve the 8th Seaforth Highrs. in the left sub-section of the front line system. The 9th Black Watch will not pass over the HIGH WOOD – POZIERES RIDGE before 4 P.M.

　　Route – CHALK WALK.

3. On relief the 8th Seaforths will move into reserve in ACID DROP SOUTH.
　　They will send an advanced party by 1 P.M. to take over all camp equipment from the 8/10th Gordon Highrs.

4. The 8/10th Gordon Highrs. will move into VILLA CAMP in Support, relieving the 9th Black Watch.
　　If sufficient accommodation can be procured one company will proceed to shelters and dugouts in the vicinity of M.31.d.2.3. Failing further orders this company will proceed with battalion to VILLA WOOD.
　　Relief to commence at 2 P.M.

5. All arrangements will be made direct between the officers commanding concerned.

6. The 9th Black Watch will take over 100% tools from 8th Seaforth Highrs.

7. Completion of relief will be reported by wire to Brigade Headquarters.

　　　　　　　　　　　　　　　　　Captain,
　　　　　　　　　　　　　　　　Brigade Major,
Issued through　　　　　　　　　44th Infantry Brigade.
　Signals.
8-30 P.M.

DISTRIBUTION.

Copy No. 1. 9th Black Watch.　　11. ...
　　　　2. 8th Seaforths.　　　　12. ...
　　　　3. 8/10th Gordons.　　　 13. Bde. ...
　　　　4. 7th Camerons.　　　　 14. Bde. ...Offcr.
　　　　5. 44 M.G.Coy.　　　　　 15. 91st Fld. Coy. R.E.
　　　　6. 44 T.M.Battery.　　　 16. O.C.45th F.A.(MARTINPUICH).
　　　　7. 15th Division.　　　　17. Staff Capt.
　　　　8. 45th Inf. Bde.　　　　18. War Diary.
　　　　9. 43th Inf. Bde.　　　　19. ...
　　　 10. 46th Inf. Bde.

Operation order no. 55
by
Lt Col. H. A. Thomson D.S.O.
Commdg. 8th Seaforth Hrs.   23/10/16

① The Btn. will be relieved in the line by the 9th Btn. Black Watch on the night 23/24.

② D Coy Black Watch will relieve our A Coy
    A Coy   "   "   "   C Coy
    B Coy   "   "   "   B Coy
    C Coy   "   "   "   D Coy

③ Guides 1 per platoon and one from H.Qrs. will be at CHALK PIT WALK at west end of MARTINPUICH at M.3.a.3.0 at 4 P.M.

④ Tools 100% will be dumped immediately before relief is expected and will be handed over to the incoming Corps. Coys will be very careful to point out tool dumps to relieving Coys.

⑤ The Quartermaster will arrange to hand over the drying shed at Byde Hqrs to the relieving Btn.

Appendix XXII
Copy No. 7

(6) On relief Coys will march direct to ACID DROP SOUTH (CONTALMAISON CUTTING) On passing VILLA CAMP each Coy will complete to 100% tools from those dumped there by the Black Watch on the Road

(7) Cooks will proceed to ACID DROP SOUTH at 5 P.M. and report to the QMr on arrival. Hot soup and rum will be prepared for issue to the men on return to camp. D & B Coys will probably arrive about 7 P.M.
The QMr will provide dry socks.

(8) Mess boxes and any surplus officers kit will be dumped at railhead dump in at 5 pm for transport to VILLA STATION — where it will arrive sometime after 6 pm.

(9) Trench Stores will be handed over & receipts taken. Receipts to reach Battn HQ by 12 noon tomorrow.

(10) Completion of relief to be reported to Battn HQ.

(1) O.C. A Coy
2 "   B "
3 "   C "
4 "   D "
5 & QMr

6 Transport Officer
7 & 8 War Diary
     & File

E S Blackwood 2/Lieut
Adj. 8 Seaforth Hrs

Appendix XXXIV

SECRET.   Copy No. 2

44th Infantry Brigade Operation Order No. 126.

24/12/16.

1. The following reliefs will take place to-morrow, 25/26th December.

2. The 8th Seaforth Highrs. will relieve the 7th Cameron Highrs. in the right sub-section of the front line system.
    The 8th Seaforth Highrs. will not pass over the HIGH WOOD - POZIERES RIDGE before 4 P.M.
    Route CHALK WALK.

3. On relief the 7th Cameron Highrs. will move into reserve in ACID DROP SOUTH.
    They will send an advanced party by 1 P.M. to take over all camp equipment from the 8th Seaforth Highrs.

4. All arrangements to be made direct between the Officers Commanding concerned.

5. 100% tools will be taken over by the 8th Seaforths.

6. Completion of relief to be reported by wire to Brigade Headquarters.

Issued through   Captain,
  Signals.   Brigade Major,
  6 P.M.   44th Infantry Brigade.

DISTRIBUTION.

Copy No. 1. 9th Black Watch.   11. Left Group D.A.
         2. 8th Seaforths.   12. Bde. Signals.
         3. 8/10th Gordons.   13. Bde. Transport Offcr.
         4. 7th Camerons.   14. A/Bde. Bombing Offcr.
         5. 44 M.G.Coy.   15. 91st Field Coy. R.E.
         6. 44 T.M.Bty.   16. 45th F.A. (MARTINPUICH).
         7. 15th Division.   17. Staff Capt.
         8. 45th Inf. Bde.   18. War Diary.
         9. 46th Inf. Bde.   19. File.
        10. 154th Inf. Bde.

Secret.   OPERATION ORDER (Appendix 51 (No 9))
          Lieut. Col. N. D. Thomson DSO
          Comndg. 8th Seaforth Highrs — Dec 25

1. The Battn. will relieve the 7th Bn. Camerons in the right sub-section of the firing line.

(2) B Coy. will relieve D Coy. 7th Cam. Hrs. in front line
    D Coy.   "   C Coy.   do   in 1st Support
    A Coy.   "   A Coy.   do   in 2nd Support
    C Coy.   "   B Coy.   do   in Battn. Reserve

   Route CONTALMAISON VILLA ORDER B. D. A. C. H.Q.

3) Guides, 1 platoon + 1 H.Q. will be at junction of Queen Bob South of MARTINPUICH at 4.15 p.m.

(4) All movements to be at intervals of 200 yds. between platoons + equivalent units.

(5) The first platoon of B Coy will move off at 2.45 p.m. No movements to take place beyond the HIGH WOOD – POZIERES RIDGE before 4.0 p.m.

(6) Tools will not be carried. 100% will be taken over from the Cameronians.

7) Rations of the two rear Coys. will be unloaded at the R.E. Dump — MARTINPUICH. The two forward Coys. + H.Qrs. rations will be pushed up to Bn.Head in the vicinity of 26 AVENUE on 3 limbers detailed for the purpose.

(8) Officers mess boxes will be ready to load in limbers which are to be in Camp at 8.30 p.m.

(9) Blankets are to be rolled in bundles of 10 with Officers valises rolled plus kit and to be deposited in No 24 Hut. forthwith.

(10) The Lewis Gun officer will arrange for one Reserve team per Coy. to be left behind.

(11) Completion of Relief to be reported to Battn. H.Q. by wire.

G E Blackwood
??? ???

DISTRIBUTION
———————

Copy. No (1) to A Coy   (6) Quarter Master
     (2) OC B Coy   (7) Transport Officer
     (3) OC C Coy   (8) ??? OC ???
     (4) OC D Coy   (9) War Diary
     (5) Lewis Gun Officer (10) File

SECRET.   7th (S) Battalion Cameron High'rs   Copy No 8.
OPERATION ORDERS No 7   Appendix 36

CHRISTMAS DAY 1916.

1. The 7th Cameron High'rs will be relieved by 8th Seaforth High'rs in the Right Sub-Section, Left Sector tonight.

   B Coy. 8th Seaforth H'rs. will relieve "D" Coy. 7th Cameron H'rs. - Front Line -
   D Coy.   "   "   "   "C" Coy. " Support. O.9.1
   A Coy.   "   "   "   "A" Coy. " 26th AVENUE
   C Coy.   "   "   "   "B" Coy - MARTINPUICH.

2. All receipts of Trench Stores & handed over will be rendered to Batt'n Headqrs., ACID DROP CAMP SOUTH by 10 a.m.

3. "A" and "B" Coys. will arrange to take back all Gum Boots and the 80% of Tools brought in by "B" & "D" Coys. will be handed over to the incoming Companies of 8th Seaforths. All Dixies, Cooking Utensils and 8 Petrol Tins per Company brought into the line will be taken back to Camp by all Companies.

4. 2/Lieut. COVENTRY will take over Camp and arrange for Guides to meet Platoons so that there is no delay after arrival in camp. The Q.M. will make arrangements for hot tea for Companies on arrival.

5. On relief Companies will proceed by Platoons at 100 yards intervals by most convenient route to ACID DROP CAMP, SOUTH. Os. C. Companies will report arrival there to Battalion Orderly Room.

6. Guides, (1 per Platoon, 1 Headqrs) will be at junction of duck boards just SE of MARTINPUICH at 4-15 p.m today.

All Guides will be under 2/Lieut. T.G. BROWN who will be responsible for allotting correct guides to incoming Companies, and ensuring that no delay takes place.

The Companies, 8th Seaforth H'rs. relieving "D", "A" & "B" Coys. 7th Cameron H'rs. will take the CHALK PIT WALK ROUTE.

The Companies, 8th Seaforth H'rs relieving "C" & Hqrs Coys. 7th Cameron H'rs. will take the LE SARS WALK Route.

7. Completion of relief to be wired by Code to Battalion Headqrs., 26th AVENUE.

A Chapman.
Captain & Adjutant
7th & Br. Cameron High'rs

Issued at 7 a.m. 25/17/16

Copy No 1 to OC 'A' Coy
     2 - - 'B' "
     3 - - 'C' "
     4 - - 'D' "
     5 - L.G.O.
     6 - Q.M.
     7 - T.O.
     8. C.O. 8th Seaforth H's.
     9. War Diary
    10 FILE

SECRET

Appendix XXVII

= OPERATION ORDER No 52 =

Major U. P. Swinburne, Copy No 3
Commdg. 8th Seaforth Hrs ——— Dec. 26D 1911

(1) "C" Coy will relieve "B" Coy in the firing line tonight.

(2) Guides 1 per platoon from "B" Coy will report to O.C. "C" Coy at 5 pm.

(3) "C" Coy will, in addition to the iron ration, carry with them one days rations and will move off as soon as rations have been distributed.

(4) Relief will be reported by wire to Battn. H.Q. when complete.

(5) On relief "B" Coy will continue working till midnight after which "C" Coy will carry on the work.

26/12/16

Adjt. 8 Seaforth Hrs 2/Lt

DISTRIBUTION
Copy No 1. O.C "C" Coy   (5) File
         2   O.C B Coy
         3) War Diary.
         4)

Appendix XXXVIII

S E C R E T.   Copy No. 2

44th Infantry Brigade Operation Order No. 127.

26-12-16.

Reference:-
  15th Div. Maps
  17, 17A, 17B. 1/10,000.

  1.   The 44th Infantry Brigade will be relieved in the line by the 46th Infantry Brigade in the left section of the Divisional front to-morrow, 27/28th, in accordance with the table on reverse.

  2.   The two battalions in the line will collect all available tools at Company H.Q., supports and picquets, and hand them over to the incoming battalions.

  3.   The 46th Infantry Brigade will take over three Stokes Mortars in line.

  4.   Receipts will be taken for all trench stores handed over and sent to Brigade H.Q. by 10 A.M. 28th instant.

  5.   All details of reliefs will be arranged between Commanding Officers concerned.

  6.   The 9th Black Watch will detail 1 F.C.O. for a Control Post at the junction of CHALK and LE S__ Trenches. He will report to Brigade Headquarters for instructions at 3 P.M. on the 27th.

  7.   Completion of relief and arrival in Camp will be reported to Brigade Headquarters by wire.

  8.   Brigade Headquarters will close at M.32.a.2½.1. on completion of relief, and open simultaneously at SHELTER WOOD.

                                   _____, Captain,
Issued through   Brigade Major,
  Signals.   44th Infantry Brigade.
  1 P.M.

              DISTRIBUTION.

Copy No. 1. 9th Black Watch.   11. Left Group Arty.
        2. 8th Seaforths.   12. Bde. Signals.
        3. 8/10th Gordons.   13. Bde. Transport Offcr.
        4. 7th Camerons.   14. A/Bde. Bombing Offcr.
        5. 44 M.G. Coy.   15 91st Field Coy. R.E.
        6. 44 T.M. Battery.   16 45th F.A. (MARTINPUICH).
        7. 15th Division.   17. A.P.M. 15th Div.
        8. 45th Inf. Bde.   18. Staff Capt.
        9. 46th Inf. Bde.   19. War Diary.
       10. 154th Inf. Bde.   20. File.

RELIEF TABLE TO ACCOMPANY 44TH INFANTRY BRIGADE OPERATION ORDER No.127.

Unit being relieved.	Relieving unit.	GUIDES. Time, place, etc.	Destination.	Taking over Camp from	Remarks.
7th Cameron Highrs. (AJID DROP SOUTH).	10th Sco:Rifles	Guides - Nil. Relief to commence at 1-30 P.M.	SHELTER WOOD NORTH.	12th H.L.I.	Advanced parties will be sent by both battns. by mid-day.
8/10th Gordon Highrs (VILLA CAMP).	10/11 H.L.I.	Guides - Nil. Relief to commence at 2 P.M.	SCOTS REDOUBT SOUTH.	10/11 H.L.I.	- do -
44 M.G.Coy.	46th M.G.Coy.	Guides - 1 per Gun in the line. 1 per Coy. at M.G. Coy.H.Q., the MILL MARTINPUICH,M.27.c.1.7. at 3-15 P.M.	SHELTER WOOD H.Q.Camp.	46th M.G.Coy	- do -
44 T.M.Battery.	46 T.M.Battery.	GUIDES - 1 per mortar in the line, at Bde.H.Q. M.32.a.62.2. 4 P.M.	- do -	46 T.M.Bty.	- do -
9th Black Watch. (Left Support Bn.).	7/8th K.O.S.B.	GUIDES - 1 per platoon. 1 per Battn. H.Q. at Bde. H.Q. M.32.a.22.2. at 4-45 P.M.	SCOTS REDOUBT NORTH.	10 Sco: Rifles.	- do -
8th Seaforth Highrs. (Right front Battn.).	12th H.L.I.	- do - Time - 5-15 P.M.	SHELTER WOOD SOUTH.	7/8th K.O.S.B.	- do -

Appendix XL

SECRET.   Copy No. 2

44th Infantry Brigade Operation Order No. 128.

Reference :-   Saturday, 30th Dec., 1916.
  15th Div.Maps,
   17, 17A, 17B. 1/10,000.

1. The 44th Infantry Brigade will relieve the 45th Infantry Brigade in the right section of the Divisional front to-morrow, 31st December/1st Jan., 1917, in accordance with the table shown on reverse.

2. Three sections of the 74th Field Company R.E. will come under 44th Infantry Brigade on completion of relief.

3. All movements from camp to be by platoons at 200 yards interval.

4. The 8/10th Gordon Highrs., and 7th Cameron Highrs. will take over 100 tools from the battalions they relieve.

5. Relieving units will march on the trench boards when passing units relieved.

6. Brigade Headquarters will close at SHELTER WOOD at 3 P.M. and will open simultaneously at Brigade Headquarters N.27.c.3.½.

7. On completion of relief the 44th Infantry Brigade Commander will assume command of the right section.

Issued through   [signature] Captain,
  Signals.   Brigade Major,
1 P.M.   44th Infantry Brigade.

Copies to :-
No. 1. 9th Black Watch.
    2. 8th Seaforths.
    3. 8/10th Gordons.
    4. 7th Camerons.
    5. 44 M.G.Coy.
    6. 44 T.M.Battery.
    7. 15th Div.
    8. Left Group Artillery.
    9. 45th Inf. Bde.
  10. 46th Inf. Bde.
  11. Left Bde. 50th Div.
  12. Bde. Signals.
  13. Bde.Transport Offcr.
  14. A/Bde.Bombing Offcr.
  15. 74th Field Coy.R.E.
  16. 45th Fld.Amb. (MARTINPUICH).
  17. Supply Offcr.
  18. No.2 Coy.Train.
  19. Staff Capt.
  20. War Diary.
  21. File.

TABLE TO ACCOMPANY 154th INFANTRY BRIGADE OPERATION ORDER No. 128, d/ 30-12-17.

Relieving unit. on order of relief.	Unit to be relieved.	GUIDES. Time & Place.	Destination of unit relieved.	Route.	Remarks.
9th Black Watch. (SCOTS REDOUBT N.)	8th Cameron Hrs. (reserve).	Nil. Relief commence at 4 P.M.	SHELTER WOOD NORTH. (7th Camerons)	L. SAP WALK.	2 Camerons now at PIONEER CAMP.
41 M.G.Company.	45 M.G.Company.	1 per gun in position at 45 M.G.Coy. GUILING, MAMETZ WOOD, K.35.A. Time - 4 P.M.	Brigade H.Q.Camp, SHELTER WOOD.	- do -	
41 T.M.Battery.	45 T.M.Battery.	1 per gun in the line. 45 T.M.Bty., GUILING, MAMETZ WOOD, K.35.A. Time - 4-15 P.M.	- do -	- do -	3 Stokes mortars in the line to be taken over.
8/10th Gordons. (SCOTS REDOUBT S.)	11th A.& S.H. Right Front line. Bn.H.Q. L.28.b. C. 7.8.	1 per platoon, 1 Bn. H.Q. at Bde.H.Q. 4-15 P.M.	SCOTS REDOUBT SOUTH. (8/10th Gordons).	- do -	
7th Camerons. SHELTER WOOD NORTH.	6/7th R.S.F. Left Front line. Bn.H.Q. L.22.b. 3.12.	- do - Time - 5-15 P.M.	SHELTER WOOD SOUTH. (8th Seaforths).	- do -	
8th Seaforths. SHELTER WOOD SOUTH.	13th Royal Scots. 3 Coy's P.U.B. SEAFISH Area. 1 Coy. 7 ELMS. Bn.H.Q. 7 ELMS. K.28.D.Central.	- do - Time - 5-15 P.M.	SCOTS WOOD NORTH. (9th Black Watch).	- do -	

SECRET

OPERATION ORDER No 54
by
Major O.P. Swinburne
Commg. 8th Seaforth Highlanders — 30.12.16

Appendix

Ref. 15th Div. Map. No 17b. of 8.12.16

(1) The Battalion will relieve the 13th Battn. The Royal Scots in support on the night of Dec. 31st/Jan. 1st 1916-7.
"A" Coy. 8th Seaforths will relieve "A" Coy. Royal Scots in PRUE TRENCH
"B" Coy.   "   "   "   "   "B" Coy.   "   "   in SEVEN ELMS
"C" Coy.   "   "   "   "   "C" Coy.   "   "   in STARFISH TRENCH
"D" Coy.   "   "   "   "   "D" Coy.   "   "   in STARFISH TRENCH.
Headquarters will move to SEVEN ELMS - Pt. M. 28. d. Central.

(2) GUIDES 1 per platoon and 1 for H.Qrs. will meet at the junction of the LE SARS WALK and the CUTTING, MARTINPUICH - Pt. M. 33. a. at 5.45 p.m.

(3) ORDER of MARCH - Hd. Qrs., "B", "A", "C" and "D" Coys; HD.Qrs. pioneers will march with "A" Coy.

(4) TIME Hd. Qrs. will move off at 3.45. p.m. and Coys. will follow at intervals of 200 yards between platoons & equivalent units.

(5) DRESS Fighting Order - sand-bags will be worn as gaiters, but no puttees. Gum Boots will be carried.

(6) AN ADVANCE PARTY of 1 officer per Coy., Signalling Sgt., 2 signallers and 1 N.C.O. per platoon will leave camp at 2 p.m. and will report to "C" Coy. of the Royal Scots in the CUTTING, MARTINPUICH, for guides.

(7) ALL BLANKETS will be rolled in bundles of 10, labelled, and taken to the Coy. Store by 10 a.m.
Officers' valises will also be packed and ready for removal 10 a.m. at Battn. Q.M. Stores.

(8) OFFICERS' MESS BOXES will be packed and ready for removal by 2.30 p.m.

(9) BOMBS, ammunition, and sand bags will be issued at Battn. Q.M. Stores as follows:- "A" Coy. - 10 a.m.   "C" Coy. 10.30 a.m.
    "B" Coy. - 10.15 a.m.   "D" Coy. 10.45 a.m.

(10) RATIONS - One day's rations in addition to the Iron Ration will be carried on the man.

(11) One RESERVE LEWIS GUN (TEAM) per Coy. and an extra team from "A" Coy. under Sgt. Hoad will parade, with two blankets per man, and will proceed to PIONEER CAMP under the direction of the Q.M. The Q.M. will arrange for the rationing of this party.

(12) Completion of Relief to be reported to Battn. H.Qrs.

2/Lieut.
7 Adjutant, 8th Seaforth Highrs.

Distribution
Serial No 1. O.C "A" Coy.   6. Q.M.
         2. O.C "B" Coy.   7. Trans. Officer
         3. O.C "C" Coy.   8. War
         4. O.C "D" Coy.   9. Diary
         5. Sig. Officer   10. File.

www.ingramcontent.com/pod-product-compliance
Lightning Source LLC
Chambersburg PA
CBHW081401160426
43193CB00013B/2084